The Chan-ese Way

The Chan-ese Way

Selected Chinese Recipes

Titus Chan

Reston Publishing Company, Inc.
A Prentice-Hall Company
Reston, Virginia 22090

Library of Congress Cataloging in Publication Data

Chan, Titus.
    The Chan-ese way.

    Selected from the author's Public Broadcasting Service
television series of the same title.
    1. Cookery, Chinese.   I. Title.
TX724.5.C5C463   641.5'951   74-16221
ISBN 0-87909-117-7

The Chan-ese Way
Titus Chan

10 9 8 7 6 5 4 3 2 1

Printed in the United States of America

This book is sincerely dedicated to the Public Broadcasting Service and its affiliated stations for the support they have given me through the showing of my series "The Chan-ese Way"; further, to those former students of my cooking classes, now scattered throughout the world, who have been such an encouragement to me in writing this book; and to the thoughtful viewers who have written so often and waited so patiently for it to be published.

Contents

contents

contents

Preface

There are approximately 25 schools of Chinese cooking and 32 methods, which are generally grouped for simplicity into two main categories: Northern, or Mandarin cooking, and Southern, or Cantonese cooking. The latter is by far the most popular and widespread—an educated guess would give it 95 percent of all Chinese cooking done outside of China.

Part of the widespread popularity of Cantonese cooking is due to the fact that the people of Kwangtung Province, where Canton is located, were the most adventurous of China's people, and carried their style of cooking with them as they spread far and wide. In recent years, however, especially since President Nixon's trip to China, Northern food has become more popular in the United States.

One of the characteristics of all Chinese cooking is maximum time devoted to preparation and minimum time devoted to actual cooking. This has developed chiefly as an answer to the many fuel shortages in China over the centuries. The most commonly used methods today are steaming *(jing)*, stir-frying *(chow)*, fricasseeing *(mun)*, roasting, barbecuing *(siu)*, deep frying *(ji'a)*, and red cooking *(hung shao)*.

Steaming is a very swift form of cooking and widely used in the home. The famed Chinese floating restaurants also frequently employ this method because of the small kitchen area available. Some Western cooks may be familiar with the dry form of steaming using double boilers in which the steam never actually touches the food. The Chinese use the wet steam method in which the food is cooked by direct contact with moist heat.

In this method water is boiled vigorously in a large vessel. The food to be cooked is then placed in an open dish suspended above water level with steam circulating around it. This is one of the best methods of preparing fresh fish as it preserves its delicate flavor. Never place the fish in the steaming pit, however, until the water is vigorously boiling and emitting plenty of steam. Even a short interval at a lukewarm temperature is enough to destroy the delicate flavor.

Stir-frying is probably the most famous, versatile, and difficult of all the Chinese methods. In order to achieve proper color, flavor, and aroma, it is necessary to master the method of cutting ingredients, the order of placing them into the wok or frying pan, and the temperature of the fire. It is most important that ingredients be prepared in advance and arranged in a systematic pattern on plates or a platter before the heat is ever turned on. The cooking time is brief and ingredients are added seconds apart. The split-second timing prohibits stopping to slice or mix any ingredients while cooking is in process.

Professional cooks use a method that is simple and can be very useful at home as well when preparing large servings of such hard vegetables as broccoli, cauliflower, Chinese cabbage *(bok choy)*, or mustard cabbage *(gai choy)*. This is the blanching or parboiling process in which the vegetables are cleaned, precut, and half-cooked ahead of time. After they are partially cooked, they are immediately removed and cooked in cold water. This procedure saves cooking time while stir-frying and also frees burners faster for cooking successive dishes—a great time-saver. This method also keeps vegetables crispier and greener. Baking soda or brown sugar is used in the cooking water to accomplish the same goal.

Other tricks to speed up the cooking process include cutting coarse-grained meats and vegetables diagonally to expose a larger area to the heat and to aid absorption of other flavors, and marinating meats in advance to help protect the surface and keep natural juices in while cooking. A mixture of egg white, cornstarch, and a little oil is also often used to seal in meat juices. The straight cutting method is usually used for more tender meats and soft vegetables such as scallions, mushrooms, and parsley.

Once the ingredients are ready, the cooking begins. A wok or pan is heated to the highest possible heat dry, then lowered to medium high heat. If well-organized, the cook then finishes off the dish in rapid-fire order. A little oil is spread over a large area of the wok and brought to the smoking point. Garlic and ginger are added if used, then marinated meats, tender and firm vegetables, liquor, if called for, thickenings, and seasonings. In a matter of a few minutes the dish is complete and ready to serve on a preheated platter.

Fricasseeing does not require the split-second timing of stir-frying and can be done more leisurely. Ingredients are first braised, browned, or fried and then simmered in stock, water, or sauce, until done. These dishes may be 80 percent cooked in the morning and finished off just before serving in the evening—ideal for a busy hostess.

Roasting or barbecuing is highly favored for its results but is the least frequently used of the major methods since it requires much more fuel than the others. It is virtually the same as American barbecuing over direct heat. The meat is basted with a highly-seasoned sauce while cooking or is marinated overnight in the sauce before cooking.

Deep frying is also very similar to the Western method except for the difference in preparation. A large quantity of oil is heated very hot and the food is fried until golden brown. Frequently one judges whether the food is done by seeing if it is floating freely on the surface of the oil.

Red cooking is a type of stewing with soy sauce. Ingredients are first browned or braised and then simmered slowly in sauce from one to six hours depending on the size of the cut of the meat. Or the meat may be deep-fried and cooked in the sauce a shorter period of time. It is the soy sauce that gives the cooking liquid its light reddish color.

In Chinese cooking, if one wishes to retain peace of mind and remain unruffled while cooking a successful meal it is preeminent that she or he realize the importance of preparing all ingredients well in advance and arranging them in a logical manner so that they may be cooked with the utmost rapidity, regardless of method. The authentic way of serving is recommended, in which three or more dishes are prepared for one meal. You must then adjust the quantities in the recipes that follow to account for your family or guests. Generally speaking, when entertaining, the Chinese believe in preparing food with portions on the generous side to avoid the embarrassment of running out!

Happy cooking.

TITUS CHAN

The Development
of
Chinese Cuisine

It has often been said that there are four great cuisines in the world—French, German, Italian, and Chinese. All have their strong adherents, and those who favor the cuisine of China present a strong case for it as the greatest of all.

China is a nation of widely disparate peoples, each of whom has contributed culturally to one of the oldest continuous civilizations on earth. In no area is this more evident than in modern Chinese cuisine—a 5,000-year distillation of the creative and innovative genius of this human conglomerate whose traditional emphasis on harmony with nature is well known.

The Chinese philosophy of harmony with nature

goes beyond the spiritual; it encompasses a belief that good health and the secret of longevity can be found in nature. Since plants were and are considered the closest food to nature, the Chinese literally have left no stone unturned in discovering uses and methods of preparation for every available form of vegetation safe for human ingestion.

Chinese gourmets and chefs long ago realized that raw or partially cooked vegetables were vastly superior in taste and nutritional value to overcooked vegetables—a fact that has recently begun to gain acceptance in Western dining circles. This realization has remained central to Chinese cooking theory and is perhaps its most recognized trademark.

The word *harmony* comes up again when one attempts to isolate the secret of Chinese cuisine. It is simply the judicious blending of an infinitely wide variety of basic ingredients and condiments in such a way as to create a desirable taste from their harmony.

While harmony is the key word in Chinese cooking, contrast and theme must not be overlooked. A Chinese chef preparing a feast is a virtual maestro, directing the instruments of taste, aroma, texture, and color into sweeping harmonies, cacophonies of contrast, while carrying through the unifying theme that lifts it to a symphony of enjoyment.

The Chinese determined early that there were five distinct primary tastes—sweet, sour, salty, pungent, and bitter. These are constantly kept in mind and used to complement or contrast with each other. Sweet and sour, for example, has long been a favored flavor combination, and one constantly finds sweet played against salt, smoothness against crunchiness, hot foods against cold, and large against small.

The chef is just as concerned with aroma. In addition to the desirability of the dish having a pleasant fragrance when served, it is of course a fact that most of the flavors we enjoy are actually food aromas acting upon the nasal passages in concert with the primary tastes described above.

Chinese chefs are almost certainly the world's masters at creating dishes that strongly emphasize texture. Smooth sauces, crisp and tender vegetables, meats that are crisp on the outside and soft and moist inside are characteristic of Chinese cooking. A number of ingredients are used entirely for the interesting textures they add to a dish, being colorless, odorless, and tasteless themselves.

No one will deny that great cooking is a true art, and in Chinese cooking the art form is always visual as well as gastronomic. The chef is always conscious of the combination of colors and shapes made by his or her ingredients on a serving platter. It is firmly believed that a creation is not a success unless it is pleasing alike to the eye, the nose, and the palate.

Chinese dishes may be divided into three groups as follows: (1) those in which one main food item, such as fish, is prepared and served alone with no more than a touch of garlic, soy, or a similar condiment used only to enhance the natural flavor; (2) those in which the chief ingredient is prepared with a sauce or condiments that blend with the natural taste to create a new flavor such as sweet and sour fish; and (3) the largest and most characteristic group, those which combine several ingredients and condiments to create an entirely new dish.

The serious student of Chinese cooking will find that throughout China these fundamental principles apply; however, the regional cuisines of China vary widely due to the difference in food products available in each area. Northern food is characterized by its use of wheat and barley while Cantonese cuisine is based on rice. Szechuan food uses both rice and wheat but is generally more highly spiced than the food of other provinces.

Basic Techniques

As we have previously discussed, good cooking, in China as elsewhere, is more than a set of kitchen routines. It is an art in itself. To master this art requires constant practice of the basic techniques.

But techniques alone are not enough. We also need to understand the general principles that will ensure the success of our techniques. The following general principles should enable you to take the right steps at all key points in the cooking process.

The Choice of Raw Materials

The art of cooking begins with the choice of raw materials. This is obviously a prerequisite for good results, because bad materials cannot be turned into fine products.

To properly choose our raw materials, we should examine them in terms of color, odor, packing, brand, etc. We should also examine them physically for their elasticity, hardness, and weight. Through such examinations, it is possible to determine their quality and freshness. This of course is necessary not only to insure successful cooking but to guard us against food poisoning.

In choosing meat for cooking, we should make sure that we get the proper cut or species, in addition to high quality. If you buy a carp instead of a yellow croaker, for example, you may find the fish unsatisfactory for the recipe you have in mind. The wrong cut of beef or pork may not be appropriate for your dish or may require special treatment.

The proper choice of raw materials will save you time, trouble, and waste and is certainly worth the effort it takes.

Preliminary Processing

Preliminary processing is cold processing, a prior step to hot processing, or actual cooking. This procedure can have a great effect on your final produce and thus should be done with great care. For example, when preparing birds' nests, the hidden fine feathers should be removed carefully with a pair of forceps. Small grains of sand should be removed from shark's fins. Mud should be removed completely from sea cucumbers. While cutting up a fish, care should be taken not to break its gall. Carelessness in any of these can make your cooking difficult and spoil your food.

Further, to make scaling of a fish easier, you may want to soak it in hot tap water briefly. Ligaments in meat should be removed or chopped up before deep frying or the meat may not be crisp. Meats that need cutting should be cut evenly to a uniform size. This will not only result in a nice appearance, but will also avoid uneven heating that may cause some pieces to be under-cooked while others are over-cooked.

In some cases, the processing should be undertaken with decorative intentions. In preparing Szechuan-style Butterfly Sea Cucumber, the ingredients should be cut and arranged into the shape of a butterfly that stretches its wings ready for flight. Such efforts will be rewarded by the admiring glances from your dinner guests.

Matching Ingredients

Some dishes consist of only one ingredient. Fish and shrimp, for example, have a powerful taste of their own and should usually be cooked without other ingredients to avoid a conflict of tastes.

We should also consider the compatibility of meat and vegetable dishes. Some vegetables are best matched with meat, some with other vegetables, and some with both. By the same token, frying vegetables with animal oil, and frying meat with vegetable oil have quite different effects.

The Application of Heat

After preliminary processing, most foods (including those to be served cold) need hot processing, the crucial step in cooking. In hot processing, the key lies in what the Chinese call *fuo-hou,* the strength of the fire and the length of time during which the fire is being used.

The strength of the heat should be in accordance with the different nature of the food materials. For example, dishes to be fried quickly in oil call for strong heat. Moderate heat will result in a long cooking time and toughness in the ingredients. Dishes to be simmered call for moderate heat; strong heat may dry up the ingredients or cause the outside to overcook while the inside remains undercooked. Some dishes also call first for moderate, then strong heat or vice versa.

Controlling the length of time the food is exposed to the heat is equally important. Some foods such as loin become more tender with longer cooking; others such as fish become tough and hard when overcooked. Over-cooked meats will change color from red to black, and vegetables may lose their vitamins. Mastering *fuo-hou* in cooking will not only make your dishes tasty, but more healthful by retaining the nutritious elements.

The Use of Seasonings

Seasonings are often a matter of the personal taste of the cook. The important points to note are the qualities of the seasonings, the interaction of two or more seasonings blended together, and the amount to be used.

We all know that salt tastes salty and sugar tastes sweet. But the results of blending various seasonings may be something completely new. There are scientific explanations why cooking wine can suppress unpleasant and fishy smells, and why monosodium glutamate (*vetsin* in Chinese) can enhance flavors and stimulate a person's appetite.

Some dishes are best served somewhat heavily salted, such as *Char-siu*—Barbecued Red Pork; others are best without much salt. Dishes heavily salted that should not be, tend to lose their freshness, while those that should be salted taste insipid without it.

Seasonings should be used in small quantities at first and slowly added to taste. If too much is added in the beginning, there is no way to counteract them.

Serving Temperature

All food tastes different at various temperatures, so serving temperature becomes an important criterion to success in cooking. Since most Chinese dishes are served hot, they should be served as soon as possible after cooking. Allowed to cool, they will have neither the right appearance nor taste. This is especially important with fish, which tastes and smells delicious hot, but usually acquires a less pleasant aroma as it cools.

There are dishes that are characterized by the sounds they emit when served, such as *wor bar,* and with these it is critical that temperatures be maintained as directed. The other ingredients should be cooked as the *wor bar* is simultaneously deep-fried. They must be finished at the same time and served immediately. When gravy is poured over the *wor bar,* it reacts with the hot oil in the *wor bar* to crackle noisily. Thus the nickname "thundering dishes." If you are slow in serving, the *wor bar* will lose its crispiness and fail to "thunder."

Artistic Arrangement of Ingredients

Earlier we mentioned that color, along with texture, taste, and smell are the key elements of a Chinese chef's art. Color and appearance lead the way, to the Chinese way of thinking; a dish with sparkling colors and an appealing appearance will give you a delightful feeling and stimulate your appetite. On the other hand, a dish that is dull and unattractive will kill your interest and possibly your appetite regardless of how delicious it might taste. Thus it is important to arrange your ingredients artistically.

Some ideas for decorating might include the use of carrots or beets carved in the shape of flowers, paper flowers, real flowers such as chrysanthemums and water lilies, persimmons, cucumbers, and lettuce leaves. The cook should use his or her own ingenuity in decorating, improving his or her abilities through watching others, studying, and constant practice. The more lively and delightful the arrangement, the more savor to the gourmet.

Attention should be paid to keeping the colors bright and harmonious, and in proper proportion. The main ingredient should not be covered by subordinate ingredients; it should be placed in the center with the others surrounding it. The subordinates should not surpass the main ingredient in quantity. When the dish is accompanied by gravy, be sure the gravy is poured upon the main ingredient and not its surrounding subordinates.

Order of Serving

Dishes should always be served in a predetermined order. Cold dishes generally precede hot.

In a six-course dinner with four meat and two vegetable dishes, one normally serves M-M-V-M-V-M; if there are three meat and three vegetable dishes, it would be M-V-M-V-M-V; and in a three meat, two vegetable dinner, M-V-M-V-M. The first hot dish should be the main course, the most elaborate and expensive on the menu. The last hot dish is usually chicken or duck, which is served with *dim sum* (Chinese snack-type delicacies), according to Northern custom.

The soup usually comes after hot dishes, followed by a sweet dish, then a fruit, which ends the meal.

In a dinner party with many guests, or with Chinese dishes being served in a Western manner, the menu contains mostly cold dishes, with only meat dishes and one vegetable dish or soup served hot. In such a case, the soup may be served first, in the Western manner. When the menu includes coffee, ice cream, or other Western food, these are served after the hot dishes.

The Choice of Dinnerware

The dinnerware you choose can either enhance or detract from your cooking, so you should learn the proper dishes and utensils and select good quality.

The Chinese often use both bowls and plates; bowls are of two sizes, large and small, while plates are either round or oval. Some foods may be served either in a bowl or on a plate, and the choice depends simply on which holds the ingredients conveniently and makes the food look inviting. Food served with heavy gravy is served in bowls; food with little or no gravy always goes on plates. Chicken and duck call for round plates; fish look better in oval ones.

One should also take care to see that the color of the container harmonizes with the color of the ingredients. Deep-colored plates or bowls should be used with light-colored foods, and vice versa, to give vibrant contrast.

Elements of a Table Setting

All too often the non-Chinese being introduced to Chinese food through his or her own efforts fails to realize maximum enjoyment only because he or she either does not have or does not understand the accoutrements that go with the dishes themselves.

In nearly all cases the various entrees are accompanied by steamed rice, the traditional staple that takes the place of potatoes and bread in the Western diet. It is the perfect accompaniment to many foods, especially Chinese dishes or any dish with a gravy base.

The normal method of preparing rice is to wash the rice several times until the water runs clear, add one and one-half cups of water to one cup of rice if you want "dry" rice and two cups of water if you want it soft. Boil over a high flame until the rice has absorbed most of the water. Turn the flame down to simmer and cook for an additional 20 minutes with the pan covered. One cup of uncooked rice will yield two cups of cooked rice. It will keep for four to five days in the refrigerator.

If you are using an electric rice cooker, add an extra 1/3 cup of water to the rice to insure that it will not be hard.

The practice of washing the rice before cooking has been widely debated. In my classes I have had M.D.s debate with nutritionists;

doctors usually maintain it should be washed to eliminate any chemicals such as insecticides, while nutritionists maintain that washing removes most of the nutrients. The cook must decide which course she or he prefers.

If you do not wash your rice, be sure to stir it up thoroughly once water is added; unwashed rice does not float as easily and will not rise in the liquid. The result will be some rice well-cooked on top while that at the bottom remains hard.

Long-grain rice is the most preferable type to accompany a Chinese meal. One should remember that the cooking method described is a rule of thumb; the longer the rice has set out, the more water it will need to give it the proper consistency. The cook must experiment a bit with each new batch to deterimine how much water it requires.

Rice is particularly functional in a Chinese meal as it serves to absorb and clear the oil from the throat and leave the diner with a more pleasant feeling. It is perfectly all right to lift your small rice bowl in one hand, level with your mouth, and virtually shovel it in with your chopsticks. This is the Chinese way.

No less necessary in a proper meal is tea. Tea serves the same function as rice in washing down any oil from main dishes as well as providing a sense of satisfaction and comfort. Black tea is particularly beneficial in eliminating the oily effect and should be served with the oilier dishes. Green tea is preferred at all other times.

Condiments on the table include salt and pepper as on Western tables, but also always include table soy sauce and prepared hot mustard.

Table soy sauce is simply a variety of soy that pours easily for seasoning food on the table. Many have the false impression that the mustard must be a particular type from China, but that is not the case. The Chinese use common powdered mustard that can be found in any supermarket. It is prepared by placing in a cup and slowly stirring in cold water until a paste is formed. Figure one-half teaspoon of the prepared mustard per serving.

An old saying claims that it is an insult to the cook to place salt and pepper on the table; I maintain that this is nonsense. The degree of saltiness or the amount of hot spice used is strictly a matter of personal taste and should be treated accordingly.

Other condiments are less frequently found on the table for

individual use but some that may be used if available and desired include oyster sauce, vinegar, and *hoi sin* sauce.

I was impressed to find oyster sauce on the table in a very fine restaurant in Hong Kong which I visited recently. This popular and delicious condiment may be served in a small saucer and used for dipping.

Chinese red vinegar is especially good with noodle dishes, about two tablespoons per serving, and if not available, cider vinegar is a suitable substitute.

Hoi sin sauce is a light sweet, thick brown sauce made from soy beans, sugar, garlic, salt, red rice, and water, and goes especially well with roast pork or duck. Plum sauce, frequently called duck sauce, is also a favored accompaniment of duck and other meats.

Chopsticks ~ and
How to Use Them

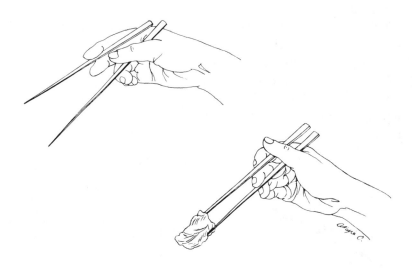

Perhaps little about Chinese dining frightens the average Westerner more than the thought of having to eat with chopsticks. In reality the manipulation of the twin instruments is a relatively simple matter that can be mastered in a very short time. Once accomplished in their use, one soon sees that in many cases they are even more functional than the Western knife and fork.

Chopsticks are usually made from bamboo, ivory, or plastic. Bamboo chopsticks are the most common, although plastic has come to be used widely in modern times. Ivory chopsticks are rarely used nowadays for any but special occasions, but their origin was one of extreme seriousness. During dynastic times, when courts were scenes of the blackest intrigue, chopsticks were made from ivory as a means to detect poison in food. Ivory will discolor, turning blue or black, when placed in contact with most poisons.

To hold, place the upper part of one chopstick firmly against the base of your thumb. Align the lower part firmly against the first joint of your third finger.

Hold the middle part of the second chopstick between the tip of the thumb and the tip of the index finger and rest it against the middle finger, as if you were holding a pencil.

To use, hold the first chopstick steady, and raise or lower the second chopstick by moving the thumb, index, and middle fingers, as in writing, to form pincers. You will soon have no trouble picking up even the smallest morsel.

How to use chopsticks

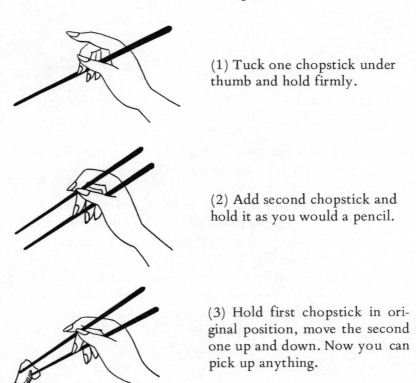

(1) Tuck one chopstick under thumb and hold firmly.

(2) Add second chopstick and hold it as you would a pencil.

(3) Hold first chopstick in original position, move the second one up and down. Now you can pick up anything.

Basic Tenets
of
Chinese Cooking

The ancient principles of Chinese cooking that we have covered briefly were never more carefully followed than in modern China today. Under the present government, a large portion of the populace lives in communal style, and the elements of quality and nutrition are of primary importance in maintaining a healthy and happy people.

Let us look further at some basic tenets in Chinese cooking theory that deal with these elements.

You will remember we said previously that it is important to select only the best in raw vegetables. When purchasing vegetables, make sure they are as fresh as possible. Never soak them in water, or leave them lying out too long, especially in a place exposed to too much breeze. If you do so you will lose some of the vitamins to the water or through oxidation.

Keeping these facts in mind, it follows then that it is a bigger mistake to cut vegetables before washing, or to leave cut vegetables lying for long before cooking. Vitamins will be lost even faster to the water or through oxidation once the vegetable is cut.

When actually cooking the vegetable, be careful not to cook the vegetable too long so that nutritional value may be retained. Do not use more cooking stock for the vegetables than necessary, as that which is thrown away carries with it lost vitamins.

One should not use a brass wok when cooking vegetables, as the chemical reaction with the brass will destroy large amounts of vitamin C.

One comment frequently heard from those who are dining on Chinese food for the first time is that the meat is invariably tender and juicy. This is accomplished by a simple trick that should be remembered at all times, especially when one is employing the stir-fry method with meat and vegetables together.

The secret simply is to always marinate the meat in egg white, cornstarch, oil, soy sauce, etc. before cooking. The marinade forms a thin and light paste, which, upon cooking, seals in the juices of the meat and prevents them from escaping.

A number of frequently-used ingredients, such as salt, soy sauce, vinegar, pepper, sugar, wine, green onion, ginger root and curry, add a variety of delicious flavors and aromas to any dish, but must be used properly and carefully or they can overpower more subtle tastes.

One would never use soy sauce, for example, in a creamy white sauce; it would wreak havoc with the color and taste as well. On the other hand, ingredients such as wine, green onion, pepper and ginger can add to the taste of meat and fish very favorably while giving off a most pleasant aroma, often better than that of the main ingredient itself.

Stir-frying is one of the most popular and flexible methods of cooking, but one should be careful to cook vegetables in this manner in the proper order. For example, round onion, green pepper, and celery should be cooked first with a little oil but no water so their appetizing fragrance may be exploited.

An old Chinese proverb holds forth that all illness enters through the mouth. In line with that belief, one is admonished never to cook or eat food containing ingredients that may have started to spoil in any way. Likewise one never uses cooking utensils or dishes that have not been thoroughly cleaned. This is particularly important with the cutting board, which should even be thoroughly washed after cutting raw meat if vegetables are to be cut next.

Suggestions for Ordering Chinese Food

The first puzzle that confronts the Westerner entering a Chinese dining establishment for the first time is of course the menu. Quite different from the menus for Western cuisines, it can appear a bit mind-boggling at first encounter.

Chinese menus generally do not feature one entree with soup, salad, vegetables, and dessert included. One orders a variety of entrees or dishes from a Chinese menu strictly "a la carte" and assembles them to his or her liking for a complete dinner. Of course some dishes can be a meal in themselves for an individual diner, with accompanying rice or noodles.

Generally a family-style Chinese dinner would

consist of four or five courses, with additional courses added if there are large numbers of diners. This is in contrast to the Western procedure of increasing the quantities of the entree and side dishes.

Let me point out that you should order strictly to suit your own taste. Dishes chosen do not have to "go together." Each dish can stand alone or go with any other. It is usually a good idea, however, to vary the dishes; for example, one soup, one beef dish, one poultry dish, one noodle or rice dish, etc.

During my travels through the United States, I have noted that most Chinese restaurants in the cities with Chinese communities use the romanized Chinese words for the names of the dishes, instead of a translation into English. For example, *kau yuk* is used rather than *roast pork*. It becomes necessary to know the names for the main types of dishes in order to be sure you are not duplicating your order.

Noodles are a prominent staple and very popular, so one should know that the word *mein* (pronounced min) means *noodle*. Any dish with a name including the word *mein* has noodles as a basic ingredient. *Chow,* as in *chow mein,* refers to the process of stir-frying; therefore, *chow mein* indicates stir-fried noodles, in this case with meat and vegetables in gravy.

Wor, as in *wor mein,* means the dish is served in a bowl, and generally signifies a soup. *Wor mein,* then, would be noodles in soup. So if you order a soup and a dish such as *wor mein,* you will wind up with two soups.

Another popular dish, *gon lo mein,* is noodles that have been stir-fried dry, with no gravy, water, or soup. It usually has roast pork (*char siu*), onions, and celery cut julienne-style and stir-fried with the noodles.

Sam see, as in *sam see mein,* is similar except that there are three (*sam*) kinds of meat strips (*see*) instead of one.

Hung tou, as in *hung tou mein,* refers to a type of *chow mein* with vegetables and gravy which also uses a variety of meats—generally *char siu,* duck, chicken, and fish bladders.

Kau yuk, mentioned earlier, is a very common name for pork that has been steamed (*kau*) for a long period, usually with taro or potatoes. The yuk (*meat*) generally is on the fatty side.

Char siu, or Chinese sweet pork, is pork that has been put on a skewer (*char*) and roasted (*siu*).

Tofu is wet bean curd, highly nutritious and tasty when cooked with meat and vegetables.

The term Canton, or a la Canton, as in Shrimp Canton or Fish a la Canton, simply means the meat is served in sweet-sour sauce. These dishes should be ordered for the end of the meal so that the powerful flavor will not overpower any more delicate dishes that might otherwise follow.

Foo yung, as in egg *foo yung,* is actually the name of a large yellow flower in China. Used with food it means that eggs are cooked in such a manner as to be yellow and tender as a flower. You should not use sauce on *foo yung* dishes, as it would obscure the color and tenderness of the eggs.

These are some of the more common dishes and terms one sees on a Chinese menu. Many are familiar. Some not-so-familiar Chinese dishes should not be overlooked, however; one can broaden the horizons of dining enjoyment by experiencing some of the following traditional, favored dishes that have no counterpart in Western cooking.

Bittermelon is a long, narrow squash dear to the Chinese. Its high quinine content gives it a definite bitter flavor for which it sometimes takes time to acquire a taste. Cooked with beef or stuffed with pork hash in gravy, it offers a great new taste treat that should be tried.

Chinese salted cabbage is pickled mustard cabbage that is both slightly sour and salty in taste. It can add a piquant flavor to many dishes or can be eaten on the side as with American pickles.

A particular delicacy is the fermented black bean. Black soy beans are fermented and mashed into a paste, mixed with garlic and ginger root and stir-fried with various meats. It is particularly good with seafood such as shrimp and lobster.

Many Chinese foods are blends of ingredients and flavors. One method, however, that emphasizes the natural taste of one particular ingredient is the steaming process. Steamed fish or any other steamed dishes on the menu, you can be sure, are simple and retain the ultimate in natural flavor. Poached dishes, such as the poached kumu fish and poached shrimp to be found in this book, are similar and likewise retain natural flavors.

One word on *chop suey.* This dish is not truly Chinese to start with, having been invented in San Francisco. Consisting of celery, bean sprouts, round onion, and very little meat chopped julienne-style and cooked quickly, it is not considered by the Chinese to be worth talking about. Many Chinese restaurants have very poetic names, but to call one a chop suey house would certainly not be a great compliment.

The dishes we have discussed thus far are primarily Cantonese. Lately there has been a strong growth of interest in Peking, or Northern-style cooking and it would be useful to make some comments and suggestions about this type of food.

Northern food is both hotter in temperature and in flavor than Cantonese food, using more spices, such as Szechuan style cooking and Peking-style cooking.

Some dishes I might recommend for trial are Szechuan-style Chicken Salad and Chicken with Wine Sauce as hors d'oeuvres; Sour Hot Soup and Four Treasures Soup; Sizzling Shrimps with Wine and Tomato Sauce, Braised Fish with Wine Sauce; Diced Chicken with Soybean Paste, Diced Chicken with Chili, Szechuan Crisp Duck, Peking Duck; Sliced Pork with Soybean Paste, Eight Treasures Diced Pork and Vegetables, Lion's Head (Tender Meat Balls), Dry Fried Shredded Beef with Chili; Creamed Tientsin Cabbage; and Peking-style Noodles with Mincemeat. Be adventurous, and happy dining!

If you are planning a banquet, a nine-course dinner for a sizeable group, or other special events, you should be aware that all large Chinese restaurants have a special menu that is never seen at the table. These banquet menus feature dishes that are not feasible for daily service due to expense, time in preparation, and other factors. If you are interested in such a special menu, consult with the chef.

Such a special menu might include some of the following dishes: Winter Melon Soup; Scallop Soup; Peking Duck with Buns; Mochi Duck; Stuffed Duck a la West Lake; Steamed Chicken with Virginia Ham; Salt Baked Chicken; Shredded Chicken a la Hong Kong; Steamed Chicken with Ginger and Onion Sauce; Deep Fried Boneless Chicken with Lemon Sauce; Shrimp with Broccoli; Crystal Shrimp; Shrimp with Lup Cheong (sausage); Shrimp Salad; Lobster with Black Bean Sauce; Lobster with Cream Sauce; Lobster with Ginger and Onion Sauce; Lobster Salad; Cold Plate with Assorted Meat; Dried Abalone with Oyster Sauce; Deep Fried Fresh Oyster; Fried Oyster with Ginger and Onion Sauce; Barbecued Squab; Shark's Fin Egg Fu Yung; Crab Meat with Straw Mushroom; Sea Bass with Straw Mushroom; Tenderloin of Mongolian Beef; Pan Fried Chopped Oyster.

These dishes are Cantonese in origin. A sample banquet menu featuring Northern food would be as follows: Cold Plate of Shrimp, Cucumber, Dried Beef, Char Siu and Cold Chicken; Chicken Tofu Soup; Red-Cooked Shark's Fin; Creamed Tientsin Cabbage; Fried Chicken Leg; Tender Bamboo Shoots fried in Chicken Fat; Szechuan Smoked Duck with Tea Leaves; Four Mixed Vegetables; Dim Sum including Spring Rolls, Steamed Gau Gee, Yellow Cake, Pork Bao; Fresh Fruit and Red Tea.

It has been chiefly since President Nixon's historic visit to Mainland China in 1972 that the Northern style of cooking has been increasing in popularity in the United States, and numerous Northern restaurants have been springing up from coast to coast.

The choice of dishes for a banquet or special occasion may depend on several factors; cost is certainly one, as some of the dishes can be quite expensive to produce. Another factor is the occasion itself. Some dishes or menus are traditionally eaten by the Chinese to commemorate certain types of occasions. For example, a typical—although lavish—birthday dinner menu might include the following:

> The peacock has always been a symbol of blessing and luck to the Chinese, and cold plates are often arranged in the fanlike fashion of a peacock's open tail to symbolize a blessing for the occasion.

> Crystal prawn balls symbolize pearls, and to the Chinese represent a wish that good things will come to the honoree.

> Traditionally the Chinese used whole suckling pig in the worship of their ancestors. Serving it on the occasion of a birthday is a symbol of respect and a wish for respect in the future.

> Serving bamboo shoots is a wish for peace of mind and good health through the honoree's life.

Other dishes have similar deep meanings and are carefully chosen to fit the situation. The chef will be able to assist you in selecting if you are unfamiliar with the traditions for the occasion.

A Chinese banquet can be made about as elaborate as one wishes or can afford. The ultimate would be the famed Ching Dynasty feast,

Birthday Dinner

Cold Meat Combination Peacock Pattern

Crystal Prawn Balls

Braised Abalone with Green Vegetable

Superior Shark's Fin in Brown Sauce

Barbecued Whole Suckling Pig

Boneless Chicken wrapped in Paper

Bamboo Pith and Crab Meat Claws in Clear Soup

Steamed Fresh Pine Garoupa

Sweetened Bird's Nest in Coconut Tureen

Baked Rice wrapped in Lotus Leaf

E-Fu Noodles

Chinese Pastries

壽宴菜式

孔雀開屏
玻璃蝦球
翡翠鮑甫
飛鵬展翅
碟盤獻宰
文昌寶鳳
竹報佳音
福如東海
子孫滿堂
鮮荷葉飯
長壽伊麵
大紅壽包

新滿漢華莚菜譜
New Manchu-Chinese Feast

午餐 *Luncheon* 菜式

1.	Dim Sum Au Choix (Four Kinds)	羊城美點四式
2.	Assorted Cold-cuts a la Peacock	孔雀開屏大盤
3.	Pigeon's Eggs with Bamboo-shoot	竹報平安訊
4.	Fried Frog's legs and Vegetable	白玉種藍田
5.	Stewed Noodles with Crab-cream	大展鴻圖生麵
6.	Fried Rice with Shredded Chicken	鴛鴦福祿炒飯
7.	Double-boiled Fresh Milk Sweet	冰花鮮奶
8.	Fancy Dried Fruits	京果二式
9.	Seasonal Fruits	生果二式
10.	Jasmine Tea	貢品香茗

新滿漢華筵菜譜
New Manchu-Chinese Feast

晚餐 *Dinner* 菜式

1. Pigeon's Eggs and Fungus Soup
2. Superior Bird's Nests with Crab-cream
3. Premier Sliced Whelk Saute
4. Fried Lobster in Ball and Chicken's Wings
5. Braised Shark's Fins a la King
6. Imperial Sliced Abalone in Brown Sauce
7. Roast Suckling Pig (whole)
8. Double-boiled Melon with Soup de Luxe (whole)
9. Steamed Fish with Vegetable
10. Boiled Rice in Lotus Leaf
11. Crystalline Dumpling with Soup
12. Sweet Fungus with Cocoa-nut Juice
13. Four Kinds of Choicest Dainties
14. Fancy Dried Fruits
15. Seasonal Fruits
16. Jasmine Tea

月中尋丹桂
百鳥慶朝鳳
加官添晉爵
龍鳳祝呈祥
紅燒大裙翅王
四頭大網鮑片
大紅片皮乳豬
竹笙四寶瓜盅
碧玉伴海中鮮
鱸魚汁鮮荷飯
高湯水晶雲吞
椰盅冰花銀耳式
席上美點二式
京果二式
生果二式
貢品香茗

新满漢華筵菜譜
New Manchu-Chinese Feast

宵夜 *Night Snack* 菜式

1. Congee with Shredded Abalone & Chicken
2. Stewed Noodles with Vegetable de Luxe
3. Fried Rice-vermicelli, Country Style
4. Seasonal Fruits
5. Jasmine Tea

網鮑金銀雞粥
鼎湖上素辦麵
家鄉廈門米粉
合時生果
貢品香茗

which can be ordered from only a few large restaurants in the world today.

During the Ching Dynasty, China's emperors were epicureans in philosophy and were concerned far more with opulence and largess than with good government. Great feasts were the order of the day with innumerable chefs creating fabulous new dishes to please their emperors.

Today's Ching Dynasty feasts are modified from the baccanalian revels of the originals, but for the discriminating gourmet they are an opportunity to sample the dishes of emperors and dream for a while.

Using a Wok

If one is to properly cook Chinese style, one must have the proper equipment, and the wok *is* the proper equipment. This versatile utensil has been used by the Chinese for thousands of years and all 32 methods of Chinese cooking can be done in it. It takes the place of all such Western utensils as frying pans, sauce pans, pots, and roasting pans.

The wok is a round pan with a rounded bottom rather than the flat bottom with which Westerners are familiar. For family use, the wok is generally 14-16 inches in diameter and about 5 inches deep. A wok of this size can handle cooking adequately for up to 10 persons. For restaurant or commercial use, of course, the woks are much larger.

Cantonese woks generally have a square metal handle on each side, much like the handles on large Western pots. The Peking wok, on the other hand, frequently has one long handle similar to that of a frying pan. This enables the Northern chef to toss the food as it cooks to keep it from direct heat on a constant basis.

The area on the inside of the wok that would circumscribe a 7-9 inch diameter circle is the main cooking area. This gives about two inches of depth, that is, the circle would fall about 3-4 inches below the lip of the wok. If one were to draw another circle about two inches above the first, this area would be called the *heating area.* Enough heat is transmitted from this area to keep the food warm, but it is far enough from the heat source that little actual cooking occurs. The rest of the area up to the lip of the wok is called the *fencing area* and simply keeps food inside the wok while stir-frying. This area is very important, and cooks should avoid the tiny 9-inch woks which have very little practical use. The 14-inch wok is a good size for every home and is most practical for all types of cooking. A Chinese home would normally have two sets of woks, just as the Western family would have more than one pot. A complete meal can be prepared in two woks with a minimum of effort, and for storing, the woks may be stacked, taking up no more room than one.

A good habit when cooking with a wok is to pour in two or three cups of water right after serving a dish and stir lightly. When you return to begin a second dish, the wok may be easily cleaned by emptying it out and wiping quickly. Otherwise you may have to scrub it to get out the dried residue, making more work and wearing out the wok faster.

If your wok is steel or cast iron, it should be thoroughly washed inside and out after use and carefully dried to prevent rust. If it is not to be used for two or three days, it is a good idea to rub a thin coat of cooking oil on the inside. If your wok does rust, use a scouring pad, steel wool, or powdered cleanser and it should come right off.

The wok, being round-bottomed, is not stable by itself. It is accompanied by a metal ring about two inches high which is used as a stand. This ring is placed over the fire or burner and the wok is set on top.

We have already mentioned that the proper use of heat is a key factor in successful Chinese cooking. Therefore, when beginning to cook, the wok should be heated correctly. Turn your burner to medium heat under the wok and keep it there for 3-5 minutes. This is ample time for the heat to be transmitted evenly throughout the wok.

Once it is hot, spread 2-3 teaspoons of oil around the wok in the heating area. Be careful to spread the oil to cover the entire heating and cooking area to prevent food from sticking to the wok. When the oil begins to smoke slightly, it is ready for cooking.

Meat is usually cooked before vegetables. The cut-up meat should be placed in the cooking area and spread over it in a thin layer to allow maximum exposure to the heat. Let it stand for 20-30 seconds and pour another small amount of oil around the heating area so that it may trickle under the meat and hasten the browning effect.

The meat should then be turned and the oiling process repeated so that both sides will be nicely browned. Once browned, the meat should be thoroughly tossed and tumbled by stirring so that all pieces are equally exposed to the heat of the cooking area.

A wok set also includes a steaming plate, which is a flat circular dish with a small lip and many holes, like a colander. This is placed inside the wok and water is added until it just covers the plate. The burner is set on medium high heat and the wok covered until the water reaches a high boil. The cover is then removed, the dish with food to be steamed is placed inside on the pan, the cover replaced, and the food steamed at medium high heat until done.

If you do not have a steaming plate in your set, you may improvise: place a small clean towel or dishcloth in the bottom of the wok; set a bowl of 2-3 inches depth on the cloth and fill it with water. Fill the wok with water until it reaches about 1 inch from the top of the bowl. Place the food to be steamed on a regular dinner plate, and once the water is boiling rapidly, place the plate on top of the bowl. Cover the entire wok and steam until done. Be sure the entire wok is covered and not just the food on the plate, or the steam will escape and the food will not cook.

When deep-frying, add 3-4 cups of oil to the wok and heat until the temperature of the oil is 350°-375°. Always test with one small piece of meat to make sure the oil is sufficiently hot; the meat should soon begin to float in the oil with many bubbles surrounding it, indicating the oil is ready and is cooking properly. Then the rest of the meat can be added. One word of caution: when deep-frying a large piece of meat such as a whole chicken, do not place the meat in all at one time or the oil may overflow. Dip the cold meat into the oil a couple of inches at first until the oil adjusts to it, then lower it all the way into the oil.

The wok, of course, is excellent for cooking soup. Simply cook according to the soup recipe as you would with any pot. A cold wok can also be easily used as a mixing bowl for salad.

Two instruments always accompany a wok and are indispensable to all forms of cooking. These are the *wok cheun* (spatula) and *hok* (ladle). The spatula is always held in the right hand if you are right-handed; in the left hand for left-handers. Both are used simultaneously to move the food, to stir, for example, in stir-frying, or to scoop out the food for serving. The edge of the spatula is often used in the wok as a knife for soft foods such as eggs. The ladle may also be used as a measuring cup; since the ladles vary in size, simply measure your own to determine the amount it holds and use accordingly. This can save time on many occasions.

Be sure that your ladle and spatula have nice long handles to avoid your hands being spattered with hot oil or coming too close to the heat.

In selecting a ring or stand for your wok, you should choose one that has a slanting side rather than a straight band. The stand may be used with the wider circle as a base or with the narrower circle down. If the narrow circle is used as the base, the bottom of the wok will then be closer to the flame.

The ring will have a series of holes around its perimeter. If you are using an electric range, wrap the ring in foil so that heat will not escape through the holes, and place the wok over the largest burner. Be cautioned, however, that as the ring sits on the enamel of your stove top it will transmit heat and possibly make a mark on the enamel. If you want to avoid this, place asbestos or some other material under the ring as a buffer.

If you are using a gas stove, you should not wrap the ring in foil, as the gas flame needs the air it receives through the holes. The ring should also be washed following completion of the cooking.

The cover for your wok should be about two inches smaller in diameter than the wok itself. When covering the wok to boil soup or water, it should be carefully placed so that it is level; otherwise heat or steam will escape. Use the cover freely when steaming or cooking heavy foods requiring plenty of heat.

Finally, you should have a pair of plain (not lacquered or painted) cooking chopsticks to use in manipulating small items such as wonton or deep-fried shrimp.

Another useful implement you may wish to acquire is a *jaw lee*, a strainer-type utensil, which is a shallow wire basket with a long handle. For a 14-inch wok, a *jaw lee* of about 6 inches in diameter is best, and is very handy for scooping out food deep-fried in oil.

Tea and Wine

No Chinese would want to complete a meal without tea. Tea makes the throat and stomach comfortable, and is considered absolutely essential by the Chinese. Although you may hear claims to the contrary, make no mistake—it is the world's most popular drink, and better for you than the water of most countries.

Most tea is inexpensive; one teaspoon will make four cups, and just as important in this era of national self-improvement, it is free of calories when served in the Chinese fashion—without sugar, cream, lemon, saccharine, or honey. They leave out the mint of the Moslems, the milk of the English, and the bags of the Americans. But Chinese tea can taste naturally sweet or bitter, keep you awake or put you to sleep, depending on how it is brewed.

Remember one thing. We use tea *leaves*. A bit inconvenient, perhaps, like the rind of a freshly squeezed orange. But how would you like to taste orange juice diluted and polluted by seeping through a paper bag? As Emperor Chien Lung of the Manchu Dynasty put it, "You can taste and feel, but not describe, the exquisite state of repose produced by tea, that precious drink which drives away the five causes of sorrow." And, one of those five causes is tea bags.

The first step in making a good cup of tea is to use good water. In general, the lighter the better. The ancient Chinese liked to use melted snow, but today one would probably be better off using distilled water. The water is heated just to the boiling point—not a moment longer. It is then poured into the teapot, which should be warmed by a preliminary dose of hot water. The leaves are then left to steep. Green tea should steep about 5-7 minutes, black tea about 3-5 minutes. Serve the tea in glazed pottery, porcelain or glass cups.

Chinese wines are also wonderful complements to a Chinese meal. Many Westerners are unfamiliar with Chinese wines, which are brewed from rice, are 96 proof, and have an outstanding aroma, all of which make them excellent cooking wines. One does not find the wide variety of Chinese wines available in the United States and Europe, but several types deserve a try by the discriminating diner. Chief among the white wines is *Mui Kwe Lu* (rose wine), and *Sam Ching* (3 brew), and notable red wines include *Ng Ka Pay*.

Soups

Soups play a prominent role in the Chinese diet, perhaps more so than in Western cultures. Chinese soups are usually divided into two categories: those which are gently boiled or cooked for as much as 3-4 hours, and those which are cooked rapidly for quick dining enjoyment.

When preparing the first type, one has to check periodically to see if more water or stock is needed to maintain the proper consistency and to draw the full flavor out of the ingredients. For example, a thick piece of uncut pork is boiled for hours with watercress until the vegetable turns deep brown and the meat and vegetable blend their flavors properly in the soup. This type of soup functions in the Chinese diet not only as food but as medicine. Pork with watercress soup, with the addition of herbs, is considered very good during the summer for preventing colds and keeping the stomach clear and healthy.

For this book we have selected recipes from the second group for ease in preparation. They consist basically of thinly sliced meats and parboiled vegetables or seaweed cooked in stock, rather than water. The use of stock increases the speed and simplicity of preparation.

Rainbow Soup

彩虹湯

(Choy-hong-tong)

Rainbow soup, so named because of its many colors, is similar in texture to American clam chowder. It is a party dish created by the Chinese in honor of the rainbow, which many villagers believed sacred. If one made the mistake of pointing at this "gift from heaven," misfortune would befall him.

Rainbow soup is easy to prepare and can be cooked ahead of time to allow for last minute preparation of other dishes. It embodies the sum total of those things stressed in Chinese cooking: eye appeal, texture, aroma, and distinctive taste, which make it popular with Oriental and Westerner alike.

Serves 10 to 12

---

8 cups (4 cans) canned chicken stock (or substitute 10 cups fresh chicken stock and do not dilute with water)
2 cups water
Dash white pepper, salt to taste

Bring the broth and water to a boil in a pot or wok. Remove any oil floating on the surface. Add salt to taste, and a dash of white pepper.

---

1 cup *Char siu* (Chinese red pork) or cooked ham, diced
1 cup frozen green peas

Add all of the solid ingredients and bring the soup to a boil. Gradually add the cornstarch and water mixture to thicken

1 cup tomatoes, diced
1 cup cooked shrimp
1 cup king crab meat, diced
1 cup *tofu* (wet bean curd),
  diced (optional)
1 cup milk
6 tablespoons cornstarch
  mixed with
6 tablespoons water
2 egg whites, lightly beaten
  with a fork

2 teaspoons brandy or *Mui
Kwe Lu* (optional)

the soup. Add the milk, then bring the soup to a boil again and remove immediately from the heat. Stir in the egg whites, mix well.

Transfer the soup to a heated bowl. Sprinkle with 2 teaspoons of brandy or *Mui Kwe Lu*, Chinese wine made with rice and flavored with rose petals.

This yields approximately 15 cups of soup.

Peking Style Sour-Hot Soup

酸辣湯

(Suan-la-tang)

Sour and hot soup is representative of the Northern style of cooking in which one flavor stands out, as opposed to the Cantonese style in which all flavors are more or less blended.

Hot in this case means spicy-hot in flavor, but during the Northern Chinese winters people usually prefer their food hot in temperature as well. Central heating is rare, and food eaten hot both in terms of flavor and temperature keeps the body warm until the next meal—with the aid of numerous cups of hot tea. The Northern style of cooking, year round, is generally hotter and spicier than the Southern Catonese style.

This dish is an all-time favorite of Northerners and wins converts everywhere it is tried.

Serves 8

4 dried Chinese mushrooms
  or a 4-ounce can mushroom
  stems and pieces
½ cup bamboo shoots

If Chinese mushrooms are used, soak in warm water for 20 minutes or until soft. Squeeze out water, cut off stems, and slice caps into thin strips about 1½ inches long and 1/8 inch thick. Slice the bamboo shoots and pork in a similar fashion.

4 cups chicken stock, fresh or
  canned
½ cup water
¼ pound lean pork
1 tablespoon soy sauce
½ medium onion, thinly sliced
  and separated into rings

In a large saucepan or wok combine the stock, water, pork, soy sauce, mushrooms, bamboo shoots, and onion slices. Bring to a boil. Reduce heat to low and scoop off any fat that rises to the surface.

dash pepper
½ cup cider vinegar
½ teaspoon salt, or to taste
1 teaspoon hot sauce
3 tablespoons cornstarch
  mixed with 3 tablespoons
  water
1 egg, lightly beaten
½ teaspoon sesame oil
  (optional)

Cover and let simmer for 3 minutes. Add pepper, vinegar, hot sauce, and salt and bring to a boil again. Stir the cornstarch-water mixture to recombine it and gradually stir into the soup until it is gently boiling again. Remove from the heat and slowly beat in the egg with a fork. Ladle the soup into a preheated serving bowl. Stir in the sesame oil if desired.

Cucumber or Turnip Soup

(Wang-kua-tang)

黃瓜湯

Serves 6 to 8

4 cups chicken stock
1 square inch fresh ginger
  root, washed and crushed
2 cups water

In a wok or saucepan, bring the stock, ginger, and water to a rapid boil. Reduce the heat to low, and skim off any floating fat. Add the diced cucumber or turnip,

1 medium cucumber or turnip,
  peeled and cut into 1-inch
  squares
1 cup fully cooked ham, diced
4 water chestnuts, sliced
salt to taste

water chestnuts, and ham; cover and simmer for 15 minutes. Add salt to taste, and serve in a pre-heated bowl.

Fresh Corn with Ham Soup

(Sook-mai-for-tuy-tang)

火腿玉米湯

Serves 6 to 8

2 cups chicken broth, fresh
  or canned
½ square inch cleaned,
  unpeeled, crushed fresh
  ginger root (optional)
1/3 cup fully cooked ham,
  diced
2 cups fresh sweet corn, or
  substitute a 17-ounce can of
  creamed corn
½ pound canned crab or
  shrimp (add juice from can
  to stock)
2 tablespoons cornstarch
  mixed with 2 tablespoons
  water
1 egg yolk, lightly beaten
2 tablespoons sherry, rum, or
  Japanese sake

In a saucepan, combine chicken broth, ginger, and ham. Bring to a boil and reduce the heat to low. Skim off any floating fat and add the corn and seafood. Cover and simmer for 10 minutes. Uncover the soup and bring it to a rapid boil, stirring frequently to prevent the corn from sticking to the pan. Stir the cornstarch and water mixture to recombine it. Gradually pour it into the soup, and stir until the soup thickens slightly and returns to a boil. Remove from heat, and beat in egg yolk.

Remove the ginger, add the sherry, and serve in a preheated bowl.

Lotus Root Soup

(Lin-ngao-tang)

蓮藕湯

Lotus is the most versatile vegetable in Chinese cooking. The flowers have been enjoyed throughout history by emperors and commoners alike and are the subject of song and verse. The seeds are used as herbs, in cooking, and as candy. The root is used as a salad, stir-fried with meat and other vegetables, used in the process known as *mun* (light stewing), and in soup. When boiled for long hours in soup, it is considered to have medicinal qualities. It may be purchased fresh or in cans at Chinese groceries. This soup may be cooked in the morning and brought to a boil just before serving at dinner time.

Serves 4 to 6

1 pound fresh lotus root, cleaned and sliced diagonally into ½ inch pieces or substitute one 12-ounce can lotus root, drained
6 cups water
½ pound beef shank or oxtail
1 tablespoon soy sauce
salt to taste
2 tablespoons sherry

Combine lotus root, water, and beef shank bone in a saucepan and bring to a boil. Simmer the soup for 45 minutes to 1 hour. Skim off any floating fat. Add soy sauce, salt, and sherry. Mix well, and serve hot.

Beef

Beef is not used in Chinese cooking with anything like the frequency with which it appears on American menus. Some Chinese do not eat beef at all due to the influence of Buddhism. However, when you order a beef dish in a Chinese restaurant it is always amazingly tender and juicy, no matter what the cut.

The Chinese never serve beef in the form of steaks as is standard in the Western world. Rather, in most dishes the meat is cut into thin slices and almost always combined with herbs or vegetables.

Out of necessity, the Chinese learned that a little beef can go a long way. It is a lesson from which Western culture could profit. Beef was scarce in China because cattle were needed to plow the rice paddies. Only when an animal became too old to work was it sold to a slaughterhouse for meat. Since beef was never in abundance, but always enjoyed, it became necessary to maximize its uses while minimizing the amount required.

Beef Broccoli

(Gai-lan-ngau-yuk)

芥蘭牛肉

When vegetables are used with beef, or any meat, the Chinese have a special way of preparing them so that they have fine texture, are colorful, and crispy.

The following recipe, both simple and tasty, demonstrates both of these techniques.

Serves 2

½ **pound flank steak**

Remove the fat and the thin membrane on both sides of the steak with a sharp knife. Cut the meat across the grain into pieces about 2 inches long, ¼ inch thick, and 1½ inches wide.

Marinade (first batch):

¼ **teaspoon monosodium glutamate**
1/8 **teaspoon baking soda**
¼ **teaspoon sugar**
dash white pepper
1 **teaspoon cornstarch**
1 **teaspoon oyster sauce (optional)**
1 **teaspoon soy sauce**
1 **teaspoon peanut oil or vegetable oil**
¼ **teaspoon sesame oil**
¼ **teaspoon salt**
¼ **egg white**
2 **teaspoons dry sherry**

Drain the meat with absorbent paper and place in a large bowl. Add all the first batch of marinade ingredients and mix thoroughly. Let stand for at least half an hour before sautéing, and preferably overnight.

Marinade (second batch);

½ teaspoon monosodium
 glutamate
½ teaspoon sugar
dash white pepper
2 teaspoons oyster sauce
 (optional)
2 teaspoons soy sauce
2 teaspoons peanut oil or
 vegetable oil
½ teaspoon sesame oil
½ teaspoon salt

Mix a second batch of marinade, doubling all portions of the first batch, but omitting the baking soda, egg white, sherry, and cornstarch. Set this aside for use during the actual cooking.

1 bunch fresh young broccoli
 (approximately 2 cups)
3 cups hot water
1½ teaspoons sugar or 1/8
 teaspoon baking soda

With a paring knife, peel off the outside skin of the broccoli, then go over the stalks lightly with a potato peeler to remove any tough fibers, and cut the stalks diagonally into pieces 2 inches long and ¼ inch thick. Bring the water to a boil in a saucepan, add the sugar or baking soda, and stir until it dissolves. Add the broccoli, stirring gently for 1 minute. Remove the pan from heat, pour out the hot water and run cold water over the vegetable until it is thoroughly cooled. Drain in a colander and let the broccoli stand at least 10 minutes before use.

2 teaspoons peanut oil or
 vegetable oil
1 clove garlic, crushed
¼ square inch fresh ginger
 root, crushed

Set a 14-inch wok or large skillet over high heat for about 30 seconds, then spread 2 teaspoons of oil over the surface with a spatula. Heat for another 30 seconds or until the oil begins to smoke. Add a crushed clove of garlic and the crushed ginger root. Stir fry for a few seconds, until it produces a good aroma. (Discard the garlic and ginger root before serving.)

2 teaspoons sherry
½ cup hot water

Add the beef, spreading the pieces in a thin layer to allow each to receive the heat equally. Cook for 1 minute or until nicely browned. After the meat is browned, stir-fry gently for another minute. Add the vegetables, then sprinkle 2 teaspoons of sherry around the edge of the wok. Add the hot water and the second bowl of marinade and stir-fry for 2 minutes.

1 teaspoon cornstarch mixed with 1 teaspoon cold water

When the sauce comes to a boil, make a well at the center of the wok, and gradually stir in the cornstarch-water mixture to make a thick gravy. Mix well, transfer to a heated platter, and serve at once.

Beef on Lettuce

生菜牛肉

(Hsiang-choy-ngau-yuk)

This method of preparing and serving beef is relatively new to Chinese cuisine. It combines the Western technique of serving shredded lettuce in salads, and the Chinese method of fixing thinly slices stir-fried beef in a flavorful sauce. The trick lies in timing the actual serving of the meal so that the hot meat and sauce can be enjoyed on a bed of cold crispy lettuce.

Serves 2

½ pound flank steak

Remove the fat and the thin membrane on both sides of the steak with a sharp knife. Cut the meat across the grain into pieces about 2 inches long, ¼ inch thick, and 1½ inches wide.

**½ head lettuce
1 tomato**

Shred the lettuce finely and spread on a serving platter. Cut the tomato into wedges and arrange on the lettuce, around the edge of the platter.

½ **layer of rice sticks, or 1 bundle of long rice (rice sticks preferred)**
2 cups peanut oil or vegetable oil
dash of salt
dash of pepper

Deep fry the rice sticks, a small handful at a time, in hot oil. Fry both sides until fluffy and the rice sticks stop expanding. Use absorbent paper to drain the oil from the rice sticks. Arrange over the lettuce, but do not cover the tomato wedges. Sprinkle with salt and pepper.

Marinade:

¼ **teaspoon monosodium glutamate**
¼ **teaspoon baking soda**
¼ **teaspoon sugar**
dash of white pepper
1 teaspoon cornstarch
1 teaspoon oyster sauce (optional)
1 teaspoon soy sauce
1 teaspoon peanut oil or vegetable oil
¼ **teaspoon sesame oil (optional)**
¼ **teaspoon salt, or to taste**
¼ **egg white**
 2 teaspoons dry sherry

Drain the meat with absorbent paper and place in a large bowl. Add all the marinade ingredients and mix thoroughly. Let stand for at least half an hour before stir-frying, and preferably overnight.

2 teaspoons peanut oil or vegetable oil

Set a 14-inch wok or large skillet over high heat for about 30 seconds, then spread 2 teaspoons of oil over the surface with a spatula. Heat for another 30 seconds or until the oil begins to smoke.

1 cup of chicken broth, fresh or canned
1 tablespoon cornstarch mixed with 1 tablespoon water
dash of salt

Add the beef, spreading the pieces in a thin layer to allow each piece to receive the heat equally. Cook for 1 minute or until nicely browned, then turn and brown the other side. Stir-fry and mix up the beef for another minute. Add the chicken broth, and when it comes to a boil, make a well at the center of the wok and gradually stir in the cornstarch-water mixture. When the sauce boils again, salt to taste, mix well, and scoop the beef onto the lettuce and fried rice sticks. Serve at once so that the rice remains crispy.

Beef with Herbs

(Lo-ngau-yuk)

卤牛肉

Chinese herbs are not only used in medicine; they are also often used to enhance the flavor and aroma of food. By the same token, some foods are taken not only for eating enjoyment, but also for medicinal purposes.

For example, of the more common herbs, villagers frequently pick cinnamon bark or dig up *gum cho* and, after washing, use them as chewing gum. *Gum cho* has a pleasant, light, sweet taste while cinnamon bark gives a hot, spicy flavor. They add the same attributes to various food dishes.

Beef with herbs is especially good since it can be served hot or cold. It makes an outstanding hors d'oeuvre when cut into bite-size chunks and served on party toothpicks, or when thinly sliced into 2 x 1½ x ¼-inch pieces and served as an entree. Herbs may be purchased from a Chinese drug store or even some Chinese grocery stores.

Serves 2

1 pound beef filet, fresh or frozen

Remove the membrane from the beef filet. Leaving it whole, pat and dry it with absorbent paper. Set aside.

1 teaspoon *buck kay*
1 teaspoon *wai son*
1 teaspoon *dong sum*
1 teaspoon *gay gee*
1 teaspoon *yuen yok*

Add *buck kay, wai son, dong sum, gay gee, yuen yok*, and white lotus seed to a mixture of the light brown sugar, thin soy sauce, water, honey, and Chinese rose wine.

1 teaspoon white lotus seed
1 cup light brown sugar
1½ cups thin soy sauce (or
    any kind of soy sauce)
3 cups water
1 tablespoon honey
2 tablespoon *Mui Kwe Lu*
    (Chinese rose wine)

Shredded lettuce

Bring to a boil and simmer for 15 minutes or more.

Add beef to the mixture and simmer for 45 minutes to an hour. (This sauce can be used to cook up to 5 pounds of beef.)

Slice the beef diagonally across the grain and serve hot or cold on a bed of shredded lettuce. (Some of the strained sauce may be sprinkled on the beef.)

Paper Wrapped Beef

紙包牛肉

(Jee-bao-ngau-yuk)

This dish exemplifies the subtlety of Chinese cooking—instead of deep frying the beef in its natural state, it is wrapped in a special type of paper called "sand paper." Nothing like the American abrasive, it is a soft but strong paper that keeps out the cooking oil while transmitting heat. "Sand paper" is not available in the United States, but aluminum foil makes a satisfactory substitute. When finished, the meat is tender, juicy, and oil-free.

Before serving paper wrapped beef, many Chinese restaurants bring you a small hand towel on a plate. This towel has been dipped in hot water with a few drops of a favored perfume, wrung out, and presented steaming and fragrant so that you may wash your hands before and after eating.

If you wish to impress a special guest, try this dish. You can do everything except the actual deep frying a day or two ahead.

Serves 4

½ pound flank steak
parsley
green onions

Remove the fat and thin membrane on both sides of the flank steak with a sharp knife. Cut the meat across the grain into pieces about 1½ inches wide, ¼-inch thick, and 1 inch long. Drain meat before marinating.

Marinade:

¼ teaspoon monosodium glutamate
¼ teaspoon baking soda
1/8 teaspoon sugar
Dash of white pepper
1 teaspoon cornstarch
1 teaspoon oyster sauce (optional)
1 teaspoon soy sauce
1 teaspoon peanut oil or vegetable oil
¼ teaspoon sesame oil (optional)
¼ teaspoon salt
¼ egg white
2 teaspoons dry sherry

4 cups peanut oil or vegetable oil

Prepare the marinade, and place the beef and marinade in a large bowl and mix thoroughly. Let stand for at least half an hour.

Sandwich a slice of beef between a sprig of parsley and two 1½ inch strips of green onion (white part only) and place on a 5 x 5-inch square of foil. Fold the foil into an envelope. Deep fry the packages in hot oil (350°) for about 2 minutes or until they float in the oil. Remove, drain excess oil on a paper towel, place on a platter and serve.

Beef and Tomatoes

(Farn-ker-ngau-yuk)

番茄牛肉

This simple dish is typical of Cantonese cuisine and the stir-fry method of cooking. It is an all-time favorite of Occidentals and is found on most luncheon or dinner menus in Chinese restaurants in the United States.

½ **pound flank steak**

Remove the fat and thin membrane from both sides of the flank steak with a sharp knife. Cut the meat across the grain into pieces about 1½ inches wide, ¼ inch thick, and 1 inch long. Drain meat before marinating.

Marinade:

¼ **teaspoon monosodium glutamate**
1/8 **teaspoon baking soda**
¼ **teaspoon sugar**
1 **teaspoon cornstarch**
1 **teaspoon oyster sauce (optional)**
dash white pepper
1 **teaspoon peanut oil**
1 **teaspoon soy sauce**
¼ **teaspoon sesame oil (optional)**
¼ **teaspoon salt**
¼ **egg white**
2 **teaspoons dry sherry**

Place the meat in a large bowl, add all the marinade ingredients and mix thoroughly. Let stand for at least half an hour, and preferably overnight.

½ **medium green pepper**
2 **medium tomatoes**
1 **tablespoon peanut oil**

Cut the green pepper and tomatoes into bite-size pieces. Heat a wok for 1–3 minutes at medium high heat, add 1 tablespoon oil and spread with a spatula. When it begins to smoke, add the beef and sauté on each side for one minute.

3 **tablespoons chicken broth**
3 **tablespoons catsup**
1 **tablespoon brown sugar**
salt to taste

Add green pepper, tomatoes, broth, catsup, brown sugar, and salt to taste. Stir-fry 2 minutes. Serve on a preheated platter with hot steamed rice.

Pork

The customs and characteristics of a country have a great bearing on its food. By knowing about the food of a country, one can better understand the culture in which it developed.

The United States, of course, is known as a beef-raising nation. China, on the other hand, has never been known for significant beef production because cattle were more valuable for tilling the rice paddies and as beasts of burden.

Pork has traditionally been the predominant meat in the Chinese diet. Many Chinese families outside the cities raise their own pigs for food, feeding them with garbage and discarded vegetables. Pork is popularly used for Chinese weddings and in ancestor worship, even among the overseas Chinese today.

Pork with Green Pepper

(Ching-ju-gee-yuk)

青椒猪肉

Pork with Green Pepper is a simple, easy-to-make dish that is quite versatile. If one does not care for green peppers, for example, the proportions of the other vegetables may be increased or a preferred vegetable such as onions may be substituted. The dish would then be called Pork with Onion.

The cornstarch, oil, and soy sauce not only add taste but also serve to seal in the flavor and juices of the meat while cooking. Browning with the extra oil also accomplishes this purpose, insuring that the meat will be tender and juicy.

Serves 2

½ pound boneless pork shoulder or butt

Slice the pork shoulder or pork butt into thin pieces approximately 1 inch x 1½ x ¼ inch thick. If the meat has been washed and is wet, drain on an absorbent towel.

Marinade:

¼ teaspoon granulated sugar
¼ teaspoon salt
¼ teaspoon monosodium glutamate
2 teaspoons brandy or cooking sherry
1 teaspoon cornstarch
1 teaspoon oil
1 teaspoon soy sauce
dash white pepper

Mix the marinade ingredients in a large bowl and marinate the meat for at least half an hour, or up to several hours, but *not* overnight.

½ ounce or ½ cup dried lily flower (optional)

Soak the lily flowers in water for 20 minutes till soft and squeeze dry. (Lily flower may be purchased in a Chinese grocery and adds a natural sweetness to the meat and vegetables.)

1 medium bell pepper
½ medium round onion, peeled
½ medium stalk celery
½ medium carrot
½ dozen canned water chestnuts
1 medium tomato

Cut the pepper, onion, and celery into bite-size pieces about one inch square. Break up the onion pieces. Slice the carrot and water chestnuts into thin, quarter-size pieces. Slice the tomato into 6 slices, then halve each slice.

2 teaspoons peanut oil

Heat a Chinese wok or large, heavy skillet over medium high heat for about 1—3 minutes. Pour in 2 teaspoons of oil, preferably peanut oil, and spread it thinly and evenly to keep the meat from sticking. When the oil begins to smoke, add the meat in a single layer. After 15 to 20 seconds, add about ½ teaspoon of oil around the edge of the wok to hasten browning and cook for 2 minutes. Turn the meat and cook for another 2 minutes.

Add the vegetables except the tomato slices. Stir-fry in the Cantonese style, using a Chinese spatula *(wok cheun)* and ladle *(hok)*, for a few seconds and let stand for another 15-20 seconds to absorb the heat. Repeat this procedure 5 or 6 times until the meat is done, and the vegetables are still green and crisp.

½ teaspoon granulated sugar
½ teaspoon monosodium glutamate

After the fourth cycle add the sugar and monosodium glutamate.

salt to taste

If the wok gets too dry, a tablespoon or so of water or chicken broth may be added to prevent burning. Salt to taste and turn off heat.

Turn the meat and vegetables into the center of a preheated serving platter. Place the tomato slices in a ring around the dish as a garnish. Serve with steamed long-grain rice.

Pork Hash

(Yuk-beng)

肉餅

Yuk Beng is a very old, very popular, peasant food. It is rarely used for entertaining but is excellent for children and older folks because of its tenderness. It is also ideal for busy working people, since it may be steamed over the pot in which the rice is cooking, thus killing two birds with one stone. Pork hash is a favorite dish in Hawaii.

Serves 2 to 4

1 pound boneless pork, ground or finely chopped
10 canned water chestnuts, finely chopped
½ cup round onion, finely chopped
½ cup green onion, finely chopped
1 teaspoon *chung choy* **(Chinese salted turnips), finely chopped** (optional)

Marinade:

½ teaspoon sugar
½ teaspoon sesame oil (optional)
½ teaspoon monosodium glutamate
½ teaspoon salt, or to taste
dash white pepper
2 teaspoons soy sauce
2 teaspoons peanut or vegetable oil

Put the pork, water chestnuts, onions, and *chung choy* in a large bowl. Prepare the marinade, add to the pork mixture, and let stand for at least half an hour.

2 teaspoons cooking sherry
2 teaspoons cornstarch
2 teaspoons oyster sauce
 (optional)
1 egg, lightly beaten with a
 fork or chopsticks

Spread the pork hash in a thin layer on a platter. Arrange the platter in the steamer and steam for ½ hour or until done.

Pork and Vegetables

(Ching-choy-gee-yuk)

Serves 2

½ pound pork, boneless
 (preferably shoulder)

Cut the meat into pieces about 1½ inches wide, ¼ inch thick, and 1 inch long. Dry the meat with paper towels before marinating.

Marinade (first batch):

¼ teaspoon monosodium
 glutamate
¼ teaspoon sugar
¼ teaspoon sesame oil
¼ teaspoon salt
dash white pepper
2 teaspoons dry or straight
 sherry
2 teaspoons cornstarch
2 teaspoons oil
2 teaspoons soy sauce
2 teaspoons oyster sauce
 (optional)
¼ egg white, lightly beaten
 with a fork

Place the meat in a large bowl and add all the marinade ingredients. Mix thoroughly. Let stand for at least ½ hour.

Marinade (second batch):

½ teaspoon monosodium
  glutamate
½ teaspoon sugar
½ teaspoon sesame oil
½ teaspoon salt
dash white pepper
4 teaspoons dry or straight
  sherry
4 teaspoons oil
4 teaspoons soy sauce
4 teaspoons oyster sauce
  (optional)

Mix a second batch of the marinade, doubling all portions of the first batch, but omitting the cornstarch and egg white. Set aside for use during cooking.

3-4 cups leafy, green vegetables such as spinach,
  Chinese cabbage, mustard
  cabbage, green beans, etc.
3 cups hot water
1½ teaspoons sugar or 1/8
  teaspoon baking soda

Cut the vegetables into 2-inch sections. Bring the water to a boil in a saucepan. Add the sugar or baking soda, and stir until it dissolves. Add the vegetables. Stir gently for 1 minute. Remove the pan from the heat. Pour out the hot water and run cold water over the vegetables until they are thoroughly cooled. Drain off the water with a colander and let the vegetables stand at least 10 minutes before use.

2 teaspoons oil

Set a 14-inch wok or a large skillet over medium-high heat for about 30 seconds, then spread 2 teaspoons of oil over the surface with a spatula. Heat for another 30 seconds or until the oil begins to smoke. Add the meat, spreading the pieces in a thin layer to allow each to receive the heat equally. Cook for 2 minutes or until nicely browned, then turn and brown the other side for 2 minutes. Stir-fry gently for another minute.

2 teaspoons sherry
½ cup chicken broth or hot
  water

Add the vegetables. Then sprinkle 2 teaspoons of sherry around the edges of the wok. Add the hot water or chicken broth

1 teaspoon cornstarch mixed
 with 1 teaspoon water
1 teaspoon oil

and the second bowl of marinade and stir-fry for 2 minutes. When the sauce comes to a boil, gradually stir in the cornstarch mixture to make a thin gravy. Add 1 teaspoon of oil to the gravy if a shiny effect is desired.

Pork with Taro

(Woo-tau-gee-yuk)

芋頭炆豬肉

Taro is a staple food in both the Hawaiian and Chinese diets, taking the place of potatoes in the American diet. You may substitute potatoes for taro in recipes such as this one if you are unable to locate taro.

Taro is an especially favored dish during the October Chinese Moon Festival, along with moon cakes and *borlook*, the fruit that so impressed Marco Polo during his famous trip to China. During this festival, taro may simply be boiled, peeled, and dipped while still warm in sauce made by mixing half a cup of soy sauce, a tablespoon of hot peanut oil, one-half teaspoon sesame oil, and a dash of pepper, or dipped in white granulated sugar.

However, the large Chinese taro, identified by pink or red short, thin stripes, is better cooked with pork as in the following recipe. There are about thirty different methods of Chinese cooking, and this one is called *"mun,"* or light stewing.

If you substitute potato in this recipe, peeled and cut into bite-sized pieces, it will take about 20 minutes to become tender. Just cook until done as you would for American beef stew; indeed, this dish is quite similar in concept to beef stew.

Serves 2 as a main dish

½ **pound boneless pork, cut
into 1-inch cubes**

Mix all the marinade ingredients in a bowl. Pat the meat dry, place in the marinade and let stand at least half an hour.

Marinade:

¼ teaspoon sugar
½ egg white, lightly beaten
dash of white pepper
2 teaspoons dry sherry or
  sake
1 teaspoon cornstarch
¼ teaspoon sesame oil
¼ teaspoon salt
¼ teaspoon monosodium
  glutamate
1 teaspoon oil
1 teaspoon oyster sauce
1 teaspoon soy sauce

Thickening Base:

1 teaspoon cornstarch mixed
  with 1 teaspoon cold water

In another bowl, combine the ingredients for the thickening base.

2 cups oil
2 cups Chinese taro, peeled
  and sliced in 1 inch x 1½
  inch rectangles about ¼
  inch thick

Heat the two cups of oil to approximately 350° and deep-fry the taro for 1 minute. Remove it and drain on absorbent paper.

2 teaspoons peanut oil
1 clove garlic, peeled and
  crushed
1 square inch crushed,
  unpeeled fresh ginger root

Heat a wok or heavy pan and spread 2 teaspoons of oil in it. Fry the garlic and ginger until light brown (discard them before serving), add the marinated pork, and brown it for 2-3 minutes.

1 medium round onion,
  peeled and cut into six
  wedges
6 medium Chinese black
  mushrooms, soaked in warm
  water for ½ hour, stems
  removed
½ cup bamboo shoots, cut in
  1-inch cubes
5 water chestnuts, sliced
1½ cups chicken broth

Add the onion, mushrooms, bamboo shoots, water chestnuts, and taro. Stir-fry in the wok for 1 minute, then add the chicken broth. Stir well, cover, and let simmer for half an hour until the pork is done and the taro is tender. Check periodically to see that there is enough chicken broth to keep the mixture from drying out and add more if necessary.

**10 Chinese green pea pods,
stems removed**

Seasoning:

½ teaspoon sugar
½ teaspoon sesame oil
**½ teaspoon monosodium
glutamate**
dash white pepper
2 teaspoons sherry or sake
salt to taste
1 teaspoon soy sauce
1 teaspoon oyster sauce

Add the pea pods and the bowl of seasoning ingredients and bring the sauce in the wok to a boil, stir the thickening base if needed (to recombine it,) and gradually stir it in until a thin gravy is formed. Salt to taste and mix well.

**A few sprigs of Chinese
parsley in 1½-inch lengths**

Transfer the contents of the wok to a preheated serving platter. Top with Chinese parsley and serve with rice.

Sweet and Sour Pork

甜酸咕嚕肉

(Tien-suan-gu-lo-yuk)

Chinese sweet and sour dishes have become a particular favorite internationally, and deservedly so. To begin with, the vegetables provide a strong color contrast and together with the shiny pink sauce make a very appetizing, appealing dish—a great dish for a festive occasion.

When the dinner consists of less than five courses, the sweet and sour dish may be served at the same time as the other dishes. However, if you are serving more than four or five courses, it should be served last. Some feel that the vinegar in the sauce would overpower the delicate flavors in the other courses, so good restaurants always save the sweet and sour dish until last to insure appreciation of every taste experience throughout the meal.

Another reason for serving it last is the belief that it aids digestion. Long before astronauts began probing the moon, the Chinese believed their vinegary sauce would transform one's digestive juices into the sea of tranquility!

Serves 2 as a main dish

½ **pound boneless pork butt,
cut into 1-inch cubes**

Marinade:

¼ **teaspoon sugar**
¼ **teaspoon sesame oil**
¼ **teaspoon salt**
¼ **teaspoon monodosium
glutamate**
½ **egg (yolk and white)**
dash of white pepper
2 teaspoons dry sherry
1 teaspoon cornstarch
1 teaspoon oil
1 teaspoon oyster sauce
1 teaspoon soy sauce

Mix the marinade ingredients in a bowl.
Drain any water from the meat, place in
the marinade and let stand for at least one-
half hour.

½ **stalk celery**
½ **large bell pepper**
¼ **large cucumber**
1 tomato

Using a potato peeler, go over the stalk of
celery, removing the tough strings. Cut all
the vegetables into 1-inch cubes.

Sauce:

1½ teaspoons cornstarch
1 tablespoon cold water
⅓ **cup sugar**
⅓ **cup cider vinegar**
⅓ **cup water**
¼ **cup catsup, or to taste**
tabasco to taste

Mix the cornstarch and cold water well in a
small bowl. Place the rest of the sauce
ingredients in a large saucepan and bring to
a boil. Gradually stir in the cornstarch and
water mixture to form a thin, pink sauce.

Batter:

1 egg
4 teaspoons cold water
½ **teaspoon oil**
½ **cup cornstarch**

Beat the egg lightly with a fork, then
combine the water, oil, and cornstarch to
make a batter.

4 cups oil

Turn the pork into the bowl of batter,
using your hand to mix it well so that each
piece of meat is well-coated. Pour 4 cups of
oil into a pan and set over a high heat.
When the oil just begins to smoke, or

reaches 350° on a deep-frying thermometer, add the batter-coated pork, one piece at a time, until it is all in. Deep fry for 7 minutes or until the meat is floating freely and has a rich brown color. When the cubes of meat are done, remove them and drain on absorbent paper or a clean towel.

Combine the meat, vegetables, and sauce and cook for 30 seconds. Stir well so the sauce thoroughly covers the meat and vegetables. Transfer to a heated platter and serve at once.

Never deep fry the meat until just before serving. Never combine the sauce with the meat and vegetable until you are ready to serve.

For an added touch, the dish may be garnished with roasted sesame seeds or canned Chinese pickles.

Lion's Head

(See-jee-tao)

獅子頭

See-jee-tao is a favored dish among the Northern Chinese, and is so named because it is frequently rolled into a ball thought to resemble a lion's head. The lion was of particular significance to the Chinese and in the dynastic periods in Peking and throughout China most palaces were guarded by stone carvings of lions, which gave a sense of dignity and security and were thought to ward off evil spirits.

Serves 4 to 6 as a side dish

6 water chestnuts, canned
1½ pound ground pork
2 egg yolks
1 tablespoon sherry
3 tablespoons soy sauce
½ teaspoon salt or to taste
2 tablespoons cornstarch
2 tablespoons sugar

Drain the water chestnuts and chop finely. Mix the pork and water chestnuts. Beat eggs until lemon-colored and add to the pork mixture. Add the sherry, soy sauce, salt, cornstarch, and sugar. Mix well and form into 12 balls each approximately 2 inches in diameter.

4 cups oil

Heat a wok or heavy frying pan, add oil, and when the temperature reaches 350°, fry each ball until brown, approximately 2 minutes.

6 cups Chinese or round
  cabbage, sliced
¾ cup chicken stock,
  canned or fresh

Cut the cabbage into wide strips — 4 inches long and 1 inch wide, put in large pot or wok. Add the stock, and place the meatballs on top of the cabbage. Cover and simmer for 30 minutes.

Soy Sauce Pork

(See-yau-gee-yuk)

豉油猪肉

Serves 6 to 8

Prepare the sauce ahead of time.

Sauce:

1½ cups thin soy sauce
1 cups light brown sugar
3 cups water
2 tablespoons honey

2 teaspoons oil
1 bunch green onions,
  crushed slightly and cut in
  two segments

Heat a wok and add 2 teaspoons oil. When the oil begins to smoke, add the vegetables and ginger and sauté over a low heat for

1 round onion, peeled and quartered

2 stalks celery cut in two segments

2 square inches fresh, unpeeled, washed ginger, crushed

4 teaspoons dry sherry, Chinese wine, or sake

5-10 minutes. Pour sherry, Chinese wine, or sake on the heated area of the wok, and add the sauce, which has been mixed well in a small bowl. Bring the sauce to a rapid boil, then gradually lower the heat and simmer for 10 minutes.

3 pounds lean pork in one piece

Add the pork and bring the sauce back to a rapid boil. Then lower the heat until it is gently boiling. Cover the pot and let simmer for one hour or until the meat is tender. When done, cut the pork into pieces 2 inches x 4 inches and ½ inch thick.

Thickening Base:

1 tablespoon cornstarch mixed with 1 tablespoon water

Strain the sauce. Use only 1½ cups sauce. In a small bowl combine the cornstarch and water into a thickening base. Bring the strained sauce to a rapid boil in a saucepan and gradually stir in the cornstarch mixture. Pour the sauce over the meat and serve. Garnish with Chinese parsley.

½ cup Chinese parsley

Steamed Spareribs

(Jing-pai-quat)

蒸排骨

Serves 2

Marinade:

1½ teaspoons brown sugar
½ teaspoon sesame oil
½ teaspoon salt or to taste
dash of white pepper
2 teaspoons oyster sauce

Mix the marinade in a large bowl. Cut the spareribs into 2 x 2-inch pieces, and marinate them for ½ hour.

1 egg
4 teaspoons dry sherry
2 teaspoons oil
2 teaspoons cornstarch
1 tablespoon bean sauce,
  canned

1 pound spareribs, meaty, or
  country style

Place in a steamer and steam for 20 minutes to half an hour. When the meat tends to break away from the bone, it is done.

Poultry

Chicken, prepared in many ways, has always been a favorite with the Chinese. Not only is chicken plentiful and often treated as "part of the family" in rural villages, but cooked chicken has symbolic value. It is used for religious offerings in ancestor worship, and with lobster as part of a wedding meat—the chicken represents a peacock, the lobster a dragon—together they represent the union of a man and woman.

Soyau Chicken

(See-yao-gai)

豉油雞

The story behind Soyau Chicken may not be as exciting as that of a chicken-lobster wedding meal, but it is a dish guaranteed to please even the most finicky of appetites and will definitely wake up your taste buds.

It is a dish that introduces four of the herbs used most frequently in Chinese cuisine; *bar gok* (star anise), *sar gen* (sand ginger), cinnamon bark, and *cho quor* (grass fruit). After a lapse of 20 years, these herbs are once again readily available from mainland China, and can be purchased from Chinese herb stores in Chinatown. If you are unable to obtain them, one small-medium, quartered round onion and two stalks of celery can be substituted.

Serves 4

1 2½-to-3 pound young fryer (not frozen)
1 bunch green onions, crushed slightly and cut into three segments
1 teaspoon star anise (*bar gok*)
1 teaspoon sand ginger (*sar gen*)
1 teaspoon cinnamon bark
half of a grass fruit (*cho quor*)
2 teaspoons oil
2 teaspoons brandy or cooking sherry

Sauce:

3 cups soy sauce
6 cups water
2 cups brown sugar
4 tablespoons honey

Sauté the onions and herbs in a wok with 2 teaspoons oil over slow heat for about 5-10 minutes. Then sprinkle the wine around the edge of the wok and pour in the sauce. Let the sauce cook slowly for 10 minutes. Bring to a boil and add the chicken. Cover and simmer for half an hour or until it is done, turning the chicken once or twice while cooking.

Remove the chicken from the sauce and with a cleaver or Chinese knife cut it into segments 1½ inches wide and 2-3 inches long. Just prior to serving, strain the sauce and pour ½ cup over the chicken. Garnish with parsley and serve hot or cold. If served cold, it should be refrigerated for a few hours before cutting.

The sauce may be used again to cook up to 6 more chickens, and after straining may be used as a condiment.

Mango Chicken in Plum Sauce

(Mong-quor-gai-kao)

芒果雞球

This is a very exotic dish which in China is considered to possess plenty of "class." Indeed it does, for not only is the taste subtle and unusual, but it has considerable eye appeal, which professional cooks consider half the battle.

If you are unable to get mangoes, you may substitute fresh fruit of your liking such as peeled peaches, apples, or oranges. The character of this dish comes from the fruit being just barely cooked, so that its fresh flavor will blend with the chicken and the sauce to bring about a very unique and subtle effect.

Serves 6 to 8 as a side dish

Marinade:

½ **teaspoon sugar**
½ **teaspoon sesame oil**
½ **teaspoon salt**
½ **teaspoon monosodium glutamate**
½ **egg white**
1 **tablespoon dry sherry**
1 **tablespoon cornstarch**
1 **tablespoon oyster sauce**

Mix all ingredients for marinade in a bowl. Add the chicken to the marinade and let stand for at least 30 minutes.

1 teaspoon peanut oil
1 teaspoon soy sauce
½ square inch fresh
  unpeeled ginger, crushed
dash of white pepper

2 cups raw, cubed meat from
  a young fryer (cut into
  1-inch pieces)

Home-made Plum Sauce:

¾ cup Chinese plum sauce
  (bottled)
Juice from ½ fresh lemon
½ cup *hoi sin* sauce
2 teaspoons sugar
1 clove garlic and 1-inch seg-
  ment of green onion,
  minced together (optional)

Mix all ingredients for the home-made plum sauce except garlic and onion, and let stand.

Fruits and Vegetables:

½ cup orange
½ cup green pepper
2 cups mango (peeled and
  cut into 1-inch cubes)
½ cup red Delicious apple
½ cup celery
½ cup round onion

Peel the orange, seed and remove the inner ribs from green pepper. Cut all vegetables and fruits except the garnish into 1-inch pieces.

2 teaspoons oil

To prepare, set a 16-inch wok or large skillet over high heat for about 30 seconds. Spread about 2 teaspoons of oil over the surface and heat for another 30 seconds until the oil begins to smoke. Add the drained chicken pieces, spreading thinly so they will brown evenly. Cook for 3 minutes and turn to brown the other side 3 minutes. Add the onion, green pepper, and celery and stir-fry gently for another 2 minutes. Make a well in the center of the ingredients in the wok and add the minced onion and garlic, if you are using them, until they give off an aroma. Stir-fry everything for a few seconds.

---

2 tablespoons water

Add 2 tablespoons of water if necessary, to aid cooking, but be sparing as the sauce should be thick. When the chicken is fully cooked, stir in the home-made plum sauce and heat thoroughly for 30 seconds. Turn off the heat, and add the fruits and mix well.

Garnish:

1 dozen strawberries or red grapes
red lettuce, manoa lettuce, or chicory

Arrange red lettuce, manoa lettuce, or chicory around the edges of a large serving platter. Dot with half a dozen strawberries or big red grapes. Empty the contents of wok into the center of the heated platter.

This should be served immediately.

Lychee Chicken in Sweet-Sour Sauce

(Lai-chi-gai-kao)

荔枝雞球

So highly regarded in Chinese history that it actually contributed to the downfall of an emperor, the correct name of the fruit is *laichi*. They are not, however, nuts as many people believe. The hard seed of the laichi is not edible, though we Chinese, not wishing to waste anything, have found a use for it. They are collected, the ends cut and then joined by a thread through the middle to make a caterpillar-like toy that is popular with the children in the hot summer months.

Fresh laichi has sweet and juicy white flesh and a thin strawberry-red shell. It is delicious chilled and served fresh. When dried, the shell darkens to a brown shade and it looks and tastes somewhat like a prune. Laichi can also be purchased canned in thin syrup and taste much like the fresh variety.

Dried and canned laichi can be found in most big supermarkets but I would suggest a trip to Chinatown where the markets are much like those in China—with prepared and raw meat and fowl as well as seafood in a wide display of choice items from which to choose.

The celebrated explorer Marco Polo was quite impressed by Chinese fruits. Laichi was certainly among the fruits that impressed him, although most likely not in the fresh form. Fresh laichi was then a luxury for many, including famous explorers.

T'ang Ming Wang, an emperor of the eighth century of the T'ang Dynasty, had a beautiful concubine named Yang Kuei-fei who had a passion for fresh laichi. Unfortunately, they grew only in the southern provinces, mostly Kwangtung, and since jet flight was not prevalent in those days it had to be brought by relays of couriers.

The lady would ascend the towers to peer toward the south, and when she saw a dust cloud in the distance she would smile broadly because she knew it meant fresh laichi being rushed to her. Fear of severe punishment should the fruit not be delivered fresh often caused couriers to die of exhaustion, and resentment eventually led to the fall of emperor T'ang.

The best laichi is considered to be that from the city of Jung Sing in Kwangtung Province. Called "Jung Sing Quar Look," it literally means the "hanging green from Jung Sing." This is from a tree that has a single remaining branch that is completely different from all other laichi trees. Instead of ripe strawberry-red fruit, each fruit has a green stripe on it even when ripe and has a special fragrant and even sweeter taste. Because of its rarity, one can buy only one at a time.

My father was a judge in that region and the whole family rejoiced when he brought home one of the green laichi, carefully wrapped and placed in a small specially-constructed ivory box, to share among us.

Laichi has found favor among scholars and poets and is often mentioned in classical Chinese literature. So Tung-Por, a statesman and great scholar, was demoted to the south by the emperor. Though very depressed, he found comfort from the enjoyment of the delicious laichi and composed a famous poem, the last two verses of which declare, "If I may consume 300 laichis daily, I will gladly live the rest of my years in the south."

Serves 2

2 cups chicken, cubed (not frozen)

Cut 2 cups of raw meat from a young fryer into 1-inch cubes. Score the center of each piece, cutting about half-way into the meat, to aid in tenderizing it, and drain on a paper towel.

Marinade:

1 egg
½ teaspoon sugar
½ teaspoon sesame oil
½ teaspoon salt
½ teaspoon monosodium glutamate
dash of white pepper
2 teaspoons dry sherry or sake
2 teaspoons cornstarch
1 teaspoon soy sauce
1 teaspoon oyster sauce (optional)
1 teaspoon peanut oil or vegetable oil

Mix the marinade ingredients in a large bowl. Place the meat in the bowl and mix well, and let stand at least half an hour.

Batter:

1 egg
2 teaspoons oil
3 teaspoons cold water
¾ cup cornstarch

To make a batter, beat the egg lightly with a fork and gradually combine with the rest of the batter ingredients.

Sauce:

2 teaspoons cornstarch
4 teaspoons cold water
¾ cup sugar
½ cup water
tabasco to taste
¾ cup cider vinegar
¼ cup catsup

To make the sauce, mix the cornstarch and cold water well in a small bowl and put aside for later use. Mix the other sauce ingredients well in a large saucepan.

1 dozen laichi, fresh or canned

Shell one dozen fresh laichi and discard the seeds, or if canned, drain off the syrup.

4 cups oil for deep frying

Pour 4 cups of oil into a deep pan and set over a high heat. When the oil begins to smoke or reaches 350° on a deep-frying thermometer, dip the marinated chicken in the bowl of batter, coating each piece well. Add one piece at a time to the hot oil until it is all covered. Deep fry for 7 minutes or until the meat floats freely and has a rich brown color. Remove and drain the chunks of meat on absorbent paper or a clean towel.

If you want the meat to be more crispy, remove it when half done or for 4 minutes and let it cool for about 20 minutes, until it is only slightly warm. Then deep-fry it again for 3 or 4 minutes until done.

Bring the sauce to a boil. Stir the cornstarch and water to recombine it, and add it gradually to the boiling sauce, stirring well. Return to a boil, then turn off the heat. Add the laichi and meat and make sure they are well-coated with sauce.

Turn the contents onto a preheated serving dish, garnish with a few sprigs of Chinese parsley, and serve immediately.

NOTE: Once the meat is coated with the sweet-sour sauce, it will become soggy if not served immediately. If you are serving more than 5 dishes at dinner or if you have some very delicately flavored dish, save the sweet-sour until last.

Hoi Sin Chicken

(Hoi-sin-gai)

海鮮雞

Hoi sin gai is a quick and easy dish with strong similarities to Western methods of preparation with the exception of the use of *hoi sin* sauce, a deep, brown sauce that can be purchased at any Chinese grocery or oriental food department.

Those who have tasted Peking Duck will recognize *hoi sin* as the sauce commonly used to brush on the thin pancake in which you roll the crisp duck skin. It adds a piquant flavor to the chicken in this recipe. One may also use this sauce, omitting cornstarch and soy sauce, for roast duck.

Serves 4

**1 3-pound fryer, chilled or
 fresh and cut into 1½ x 3-
 inch pieces**
¼ cup *hoi sin* **sauce**
¼ cup plum sauce
¼ cup soy sauce
**4-6 pieces of thinly sliced
 fresh ginger root (optional)**
juice of 1 fresh lemon
3 tablespoons cornstarch
1 tomato cut in wedges
⅓ cup parsley

Mix all the ingredients thoroughly in a bowl and marinate for 1 hour. Bake the chicken at 375° for 35 minutes or until tender. Garnish with Chinese parsley and sliced tomato wedges.

Roast Chicken with Yuen See Sauce

(Yuen-see-gook-gai)

原豉醬焗雞

Serves 2 to 4

**1 3-pound fryer, whole (not
 frozen)**
½ tablespoon soy sauce
1 teaspoon honey
½ teaspoon salt

Rinse the chicken and pat dry with absorbent paper towels. Combine the soy sauce, honey, salt, *heong liu fun*, and lemon juice, and rub the mixture into the skin of fryer.

¼ **teaspoon** *heong liu fun*
(Chinese five spice powder)
Juice from ½ **small lemon**

---

3 tablespoons *yuen see* **sauce**
 (yellow bean sauce)
1 tablespoon sherry
2 cloves garlic, finely
 chopped
1 teaspoon light brown sugar
2 green onions cut in 4-inch
 pieces, white and green por-
 tions
1 cup Chinese parsley cut in
 2-inch lengths (optional)

Combine the *yuen see* sauce, sherry, garlic, sugar, green onion, and parsley. Rub the inside cavity of the chicken, leaving any remaining ingredients inside the chicken as a stuffing.

¼ **cup green onions,**
 chopped for garnish

Let the chicken, with the mixture, stand approximately 15 minutes then place in a baking pan and roast 50 minutes at 350°. Cut chicken in pieces approximately 1½ x 3 inches. Garnish with chopped green onions.

Pineapple Chicken

(Bor-lor-gai)

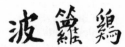

波籮鷄

Serves 2 to 4 as a side dish

1½ pounds raw chicken
 meat (approximately
 3-pound fresh fryer)

Marinade:

1 teaspoon cornstarch
1 teaspoon salt
2 teaspoons cold water
2 teaspoons soy sauce

Cut the meat into bite-size pieces and marinate in a mixture of the cornstarch, salt, water, and soy sauce for at least ½ hour.

3 tablespoons oil
1 cup onions, sliced
2 cups celery, sliced
6 water chestnuts, sliced

Heat a wok or heavy frying pan, add 1 tablespoon oil and stir-fry the onions, celery, and water chestnuts for 2 minutes. Remove from the heat and put aside.

½ cup pineapple tidbits
4 tablespoons pineapple juice

Heat 2 tablespoons oil and stir-fry the chicken for 10 minutes. Add the vegetables, pineapple, and pineapple juice and cook 15 seconds, being careful not to overcook the vegetables.

Cold Chicken with Ginger-Onion Sauce

葱油雞

(Chung-yau-gai)

One of the most popular and sought-after Chinese dishes is this recipe, which can be easily prepared anywhere, as the ingredients are readily accessible.

Since it can be served cold or at room temperature, it may be prepared ahead of time, thus allowing the cook to take care of last minute details for other dishes or to dress for entertaining. The dish may also be prepared in the morning, left to cool in the refrigerator, and served immediately after coming home for dinner. It is a favorite in Hawaii and elsewhere for wedding receptions and nine-course dinners.

Serves 2

green onion leaves and roots
2 square inches fresh ginger, unpeeled and crushed with a heavy knife
1 bunch green onion, crushed and cut into two segments

Fill a large, heavy pot with enough hot tap water to cover the chicken by at least 2 inches. Add crushed green onion leaves and roots which have been washed, and the unpeeled ginger. Cover and bring to a rapid boil.

1 3-pound fresh whole fryer
(chicken pieces cannot be
substituted)

Remove giblets from cavity of chicken. Holding the chicken by a wing or the neck, dip it into the boiling water for 3 seconds, remove and let cool for 5 seconds. Repeat this process 5 times. This insures that the chicken skin will not break up later, allowing juices to escape too fast. Bring the water to a fast boil again and immerse the whole chicken. Cover, bring water to a boil, and turn heat off. Let the chicken stand for 30 minutes without removing the cover.

1½ cups finely chopped
green onions, (both white
and green portions)
1 square inch fresh ginger,
peeled and finely chopped
1 teaspoon monosodium
glutamate
1 teaspoon salt
1 teaspoon sesame oil
(optional)
2 teaspoons brandy, sherry,
or Chinese rose wine
¾ cup peanut oil, heated in
a small pan to 350° and set
aside to cool
¼ teaspoon white pepper

Meanwhile, begin making the ginger-onion sauce. Mix the chopped onion, chopped ginger, monosodium glutamate, wine, salt, white pepper, and sesame oil well. Let stand for at least 10 minutes to let the salt and monosodium glutamate dissolve. Then mix in the cooled peanut oil.

2 teaspoons vegetable oil

Examine to see if the chicken is done. It should be floating freely on the surface and the skin around the knee and wing should be slightly broken. Use a fork to prick the thigh to see whether the juices run out pinkish in color. The juice will not be pinkish if the chicken is done. Remove chicken and put into another pot, running cold water over it. The chicken should be completely submerged to prevent it from turning yellow, to prevent the skin from breaking up, and, most important, to stop the chicken from cooking. This will take approximately 10 minutes. When it is cooled inside and out, pat it dry with a paper towel and rub the whole bird with vegetable oil. Refrigerate the chicken for a few hours. Save the water in which the chicken was cooked to use for the vegetables.

Cut the chicken into pieces about 1-inch x 2 inches. (Never refrigerate the chicken overnight). Just before serving, stir up the sauce again and spread evenly over the chicken. Serve immediately as the taste of the chicken will be at its best for only 15-20 minutes.

1 pound *gai choy* **(mustard cabbage),** *won bok* **(Chinese cabbage), or frozen broccoli (thawed)**

Cut the *gai choy* or *won bok* into 2-inch pieces. Bring the water in which the chicken was cooked to a boil and cook the vegetables in it for one minute. Drain and let cool. Cook the broccoli the same way.

Arrange the greens on a platter and top with the chicken.

Chicken with Ham

(Yin-yen-gai)

駕鸯雞

This dish has highly romantic connotations and is generally served at weddings, for anniversaries, or at a candlelight dinner for two. *Yin yen* is a Chinese wild duck that closely resembles American wild ducks but is about a third smaller, (with very beautiful feathers). Upon reaching maturity, *yin yen* mate for life. They are always seen in pairs, frequently swimming under the Chinese weeping willows near stream banks. When sleeping, they twine their necks together so that if danger comes, one can quickly alert the other.

Hunters consider *yin yen* a prize kill, yet are filled with regret for shooting them. When one bird is shot, its mate will instinctively fly away immediately but within minutes, knowing danger still exists, it will nevertheless return to the side of the dead or wounded bird. The *yin yen* is believed by the Chinese to want to die with its mate.

Throughout the centuries poets have praised *yin yen* for its love and faithfulness. A favorite subject for painters, likenesses of *yin yen* are frequently hung in place of other scrolls during wedding festivities in upper-class homes.

Those in the culinary field wished to honor the birds as well, and created this dish using unseasoned chicken and ham, blending tastes to show dependence and enhancement, one of the other. Therefore, when it is served the ingredients should be eaten together and not just a single piece of ham or chicken alone.

If you are single, serve this to your loved one with soft music and candlelight. When you tell the story of *yin yen* you may shortly find yourself single no more! Happy hunting!

Serves 2

1 3-pound fryer, whole, fresh
2 teaspoons vegetable oil

Fill a large, heavy pot with enough hot tap water to cover the chicken by at least 2 inches. Cover and bring to a rapid boil. Remove giblets from cavity of chicken. Holding the chicken by a wing or the neck, dip it into the boiling water for 3 seconds, remove and let cool for 5 seconds. Repeat this process 5 times. This insures that the chicken skin will not break up later, allowing juices to escape too fast. Bring the water to a fast boil again and immerse the whole chicken. Cover, bring to a boil, and turn heat off. Cool the chicken with tap water. Dry at room temperature or with a paper towel and rub with oil. Save the water in which the chicken was cooked to use for the vegetables. Cut the chicken into pieces approximately 1½ x 3 inches, bones and all.

8-10 ounces fully cooked smoked ham, preferably Virginia ham

Cut the ham into slices about the same size as the chicken pieces, about 1/8 inch thick.

---

1 pound *gai choy* **(mustard cabbage), or frozen broccoli (thawed) or French green beans**

Cut the *gai choy*, broccoli, or green beans into 2-inch pieces. Bring the water in which the chicken was cooked to a boil and cook the vegetables in it for 1 minute. Drain and let cool.

Sauce:

2 teaspoons vegetable oil
2 tablespoons chopped green onion
2 tablespoons chopped fresh ginger root
2 cups chicken broth
½ teaspoon sugar
½ teaspoon sesame oil
½ teaspoon salt or to taste
½ teaspoon monosodium glutamate
dash of white pepper
2 teaspoons oyster sauce
2 teaspoons soy sauce
2 teaspoons cornstarch mixed with 2 tablespoons water
2 teaspoons *Mui Kwe Lu*

To prepare the sauce, heat the wok, add vegetable oil, then add the green onions and ginger. When browned slightly, add chicken broth. Bring to a boil. Warm the chicken and ham at this point by pouring the boiling sauce mixture over them. Drain the mixture back into the pot and repeat the process 4 or 5 times, ending with all of the sauce mixture back in the pot. Then add the remaining sauce ingredients, except the cornstarch mixture. When the contents again reach a boil, gradually stir in the cornstarch mixture. Turn off the heat and when boiling has subsided add 2 teaspoons *Mui Kwe Lu*.

Use the vegetable as the base, top it with the chicken pieces (skin side up), and top each chicken piece with a ham slice.

Do not add the sauce to the chicken until the dinner is ready to be served.

Crispy Duck

(Chi-pi-op)

脆皮鴨

Everyone has heard of the famed Chinese delicacy, Peking Duck. Unfortunately, preparation takes so long (two days) and is so involved that it is not practical for the average home cook. This recipe, however, can be accomplished much more easily and rapidly and possesses many of the characteristics of its more glamorous cousin. Impress your friends with this one.

Serves 4

1 4-pound duck, fresh or frozen
1 bunch of green onions, crushed
2 square inches fresh ginger (optional)
3 or 4 cloves of garlic, peeled and crushed
4 pieces star anise, crushed (optional)

Thaw the duck completely if frozen. Cut off and discard neck skin and fat, and remove wings at the joints. Wash the green onions, roots and all, and crush with a cleaver. Wash unpeeled ginger and crush with cleaver. Crush the garlic. Crush the star anise in a paper towel to prevent scattering.

2 teaspoons oil
1 medium round onion, peeled and quartered
2-3 teaspoons *Mui Kwe Lu* (**Chinese wine**) **or dry sherry or brandy**

Heat a wok. Spread 2 teaspoons oil over a large area. With the heat low, slowly sauté the garlic, ginger, star anise, green onions, and round onion together for 10-15 minutes. After stir-frying, turn heat to high and mound all the vegetables in the center of the wok. Add 2-3 teaspoons *Mui Kwe Lu* or dry sherry. Then add enough hot tap water to cover the duck by 1 inch or more. Bring the water to a boil and drop in the duck, belly-first. Bring water back to a rapid boil, then reduce to a gentle boil. Cover and continue to boil for 45 minutes to 1 hour or until tender. Prick the thigh with a fork—if the juices are still pinkish, the duck should cook longer, but do not overcook.

Remove the duck from the liquid and cool at room temperature. Leave the cavity up. After the duck is cooled, place on a plate and run a knife along the side of the backbone. Press the duck down, then run the thumb under the skin. Break off the legs at the joints and remove the bones. Open up the duck and remove the skeleton by hand. Remove any loose pieces of bone, leaving the meat with the skin.

---

2 small eggs, lightly beaten
1 cup cornstarch

Place all the duck meat on a round, shallow plate and press into a round shape. Beat 2 eggs and pat on both sides of the meat. Press in ½ cup of cornstarch on one side of the duck. Make sure the edges are covered with the egg and cornstarch mixture, as they hold the duck together. Place another round, flat dish over the duck. Turn it over and apply the remainder of the eggs and cornstarch to the other side. Press it with the plate to make it flat and stiff. Refrigerate for at least 2 hours, or overnight, if possible, to insure crispiness.

3-4 cups oil for deep-fat frying
salt to taste

Heat the oil in a wok or frying pan. Remove the duck from refrigerator and shake off any loose cornstarch. Adjust duck to the heat in pan by gradually immersing it in the hot oil an inch at a time. Fry one side of the duck for about five minutes, then fry the other side, immersed in the oil. When it floats and is golden brown, it is done. Place duck on absorbent paper on a platter and cover with more absorbent paper to drain excess oil. Sprinkle with salt to taste, while duck is still hot. Slice the duck into 1 x 2-inch rectangles and serve, either alone or with buns, such as Parker House rolls, for instance. Cut an opening in the roll and place a piece of duck inside.

Roast Turkey in Wor Bar Sauce

(For-gai-wor-bar-jup)

火雞窩巴汁

In the old days, ovens were very uncommon in Chinese homes and turkeys have never been raised in large numbers as a food source in China, being a native American bird. Just a few years ago, however, about ten top-ranking Chinese chefs in Hong Kong pooled their talents and came up with some very interesting turkey dishes. Since then, recipes for turkey have become the "talk of the town," as many Chinese simply did not believe that the traditional stir-fry method could be used to do a turkey without first looking up a dentist.

This recipe, with a touch of Northern influence, has become a favorite of my cooking classes. With its simplicity and unusual flavor, it would give a different flair to your Thanksgiving or Christmas table.

Serves 2

3 cups roasted boneless turkey cut into 1½-inch pieces, skin and all
1 tablespoon oyster sauce
2 teaspoons soy sauce
dash white pepper
1 teaspoon oil

Marinate the turkey in a large bowl with oyster sauce, soy sauce, dash white pepper, and oil for ½ to 2 hours.

1 small round onion **1 small green pepper** **1 small carrot**	Cut the round onion and green pepper into 1½-inch pieces. Peel and cut the carrot into thin slices.
2 teaspoons cornstarch **2 teaspoons water** *Sauce:* **½ cup homemade turkey stock or chicken broth** **¼ cup catsup** **½ teaspoon tabasco sauce** **2 teaspoons Worcestershire sauce** **½ teaspoon sesame oil** **1 teaspoon sugar** **dash white pepper** **1 teaspoon monosodium glutamate** **1 teaspoon vegetable oil** **1 teaspoon oyster sauce**	In a small bowl, combine 2 teaspoons cornstarch with the same amount of water for a thickening base and set aside. Prepare the sauce, mixing it well in a small bowl.
2 teaspoons oil	Heat 1 or 2 teaspoons oil in a heavy skillet or Chinese wok over a medium high heat. When it begins to smoke, stir in the vegetables and fry for a minute until they give out a nice aroma. Take the vegetables out. Add another 2 teaspoons or so of oil to the wok, add the turkey meat and stir-fry for 3 or 4 minutes or until thoroughly heated. Mix in the vegetables. Pour the sauce into the wok. Stir-fry the meat and the vegetables and wait until the sauce comes to a boil. Stir up the thickening base to recombine it, and mix it in to thicken the sauce. Add 1 teaspoon of oil for a shiny effect if so desired. Transfer the whole contents at once onto a preheated platter.

Turkey in Sweet-Sour Sauce

(Tim-sin-for-gai)

甜酸火雞

The Chinese have a philosophy for the seasons of heavy eating—Thanksgiving, Christmas, New Year's, etc. They believe it is good to include some sweet and sour dishes since the vinegary effect will do wonders for a person's appetite and digestion. The following recipe is not one of the easiest in this book, but try it for something different and impressive.

Serves 2

Marinade:

¼ **teaspoon sugar**
¼ **teaspoon sesame oil**
¼ **teaspoon salt**
¼ **teaspoon monosodium glutamate**
½ **egg (yolk and white)**
dash of white pepper
2 **teaspoons dry sherry**
1 **teaspoon cornstarch**
1 **teaspoon oil**
1 **teaspoon oyster sauce**
1 **teaspoon soy sauce**

½ **pound roasted or fully cooked boneless turkey meat, cut in 1½-inch pieces**

Mix all ingredients for the marinade in a bowl. Drain any water from the meat, place in the marinade and let stand for at least one-half hour.

½ **stalk celery**
½ **large bell pepper**
¼ **large cucumber**
1 **tomato**

Using a potato peeler go over the stalk of celery, removing the tough strings. Cut all the vegetables into 1-inch cubes.

Sauce:

⅓ **cup sugar**
⅓ **cup cider vinegar**
⅓ **cup water**

Prepare the sauce. Mix the cornstarch and cold water well in a small bowl and set aside. Place the rest of the sauce ingredients in a large saucepan and bring to a boil.

1 tablespoon cornstarch
1 tablespoon cold water

Batter:

1 egg
4 teaspoons cold water
½ teaspoon oil
½ cup cornstarch

4 cups vegetable oil

Gradually stir in the cornstarch and water mixture to form a thin, pink sauce.

Beat the egg lightly with a fork, then combine the remaining ingredients to make a batter. The batter will be thick and may have to be thinned with a little water to the desired consistency.

Turn the turkey into the bowl of batter and mix well so that each piece of meat is well coated. Pour 4 cups of oil into a pan and set over a high heat. When the oil just begins to smoke, or reaches 350° on a deep-frying thermometer, add the batter-coated turkey one piece at a time until it is it is all in. Deep fry for 7 minutes or until the meat floats freely and has a rich brown color. When the cubes of meat are done, remove them and drain on absorbent paper or a clean towel.

Combine the meat, vegetables, and sauce and cook 30 seconds. Stir well so that the sauce thoroughly covers the meat and vegetables. Transfer the contents onto a heated platter and serve at once. For a holiday atmosphere, decorate the dish by placing about a dozen deep fried won ton on the edge of the serving platter.

Seafood

"Eat in Canton" is a famous old Chinese saying. And it is sound advice, for the city of Canton, located at the mouth of the Pearl River, 40 miles from Hong Kong, is the home of a cooking style famed the world over.

Of its thousands of delicacies, its treatment of seafood is especially favored and such special soups as shark's fin and dried scallop are internationally known and appreciated. Many visitors to Hong Kong have enjoyed dining in a colorful floating restaurant where they selected a live fish and minutes later were enjoying its succulent flavor. These restaurants are indeed expert purveyors of the Cantonese methods of cooking fish.

As a consultant for the East-West Center on the campus of the University of Hawaii in Honolulu, a few years ago, I was charged with developing recipes and training cooks in the Oriental cuisine. I compiled 150 recipes covering eight or ten Asian countries. I visited library after library to research methods of cooking fish quickly and simply after the manner of these floating restaurants. Unfortunately, books on Chinese cooking available to the public today still fail to teach this method and omit recipes that utilize it. The Chinese believe that a fish swimming in water epitomizes happiness. So fish is always served at Chinese wedding feasts and other happy occasions to connote a wish of good fortune and happiness. It is also often served at a farewell or friendship dinner to emphasize that friendship is like a fish in water—happy and memorable. memorable.

While frequenting the floating restaurants in Canton during my early college career, I acquired the following recipe which I would like to share with you. It requires no special equipment or preparation; yet it is excellent for entertaining because of its simplicity. Those of you who enjoy seafood but do not enjoy cleaning up afterward should be especially interested in trying this recipe for poached fish.

Poached Mullet

(Jing-yu)

蒸魚

Serves 2

1½ pounds mullet, sea bass, trout, or any other fish that is of good quality and does not have many small bones

Clean the fish but leave on the head and tail. Lay it on a chopping board and with a knife score the body of the fish making one row of diagonal cuts about 2 inches apart and 1 inch deep from head to tail. Repeat on the other side.

Cooking liquid:

**10 cups hot water
2 square inches fresh ginger root or 1 tablespoon powdered ginger**

Pour the water into a 14-inch wok or other heavy pan big enough to hold the fish. Crush the ginger root, parsley, and green onions with a heavy knife and add to the

1 bunch of Chinese parsley (optional)
4 green onion stalks

water, bringing it to a boil. If ginger powder is used, add onion that has been quartered. Let the water boil for 10 minutes.

Put the fish in the water, making sure that it is covered by at least ½-inch of water. When the water comes back to a boil, lower the temperature gradually so that it continues to boil very gently. Cook uncovered for 15 to 20 minutes. With a fork, prick the meaty part of the fish—if it breaks off easily, the fish is done. Transfer the fish immediately to a heated platter and discard the stock.

Sauce:

¼ cup peanut oil or vegetable oil
¾ cup soy sauce

While the fish is cooking, heat the oil for the sauce in a saucepan until it reaches 350° or begins to smoke. Remove from heat.

Pour the oil first, then the soy sauce over the fish, covering the broken skin with Chinese parsley or green onions cut in 2-inch strips. Serve immediately with steamed long grain rice and hot tea.

NOTE: The correct Chinese style is to use a fork and spoon: the fork to break off the desired serving, and the spoon to lift the fish onto the plate, and for dipping sauce to place on fish.

Spooning some of the sauce over the steamed rice has long been enjoyed by many Orientals and Westerners. However, in China this would be considered very poor table manners, as well as an insult to your hostess. You might compliment your hostess on the delicious sauce and ask for permission to put some on your rice. If she agrees, then it is acceptable to put extra sauce on your rice. Be sure to ask first!

Crisp Sweet-Sour Fish

(So-jar-tim-suan-yu)

酥炸甜酸魚

This recipe is typical of the Northern or Peking style of cooking. The method used is generally referred to as "hung sui" or "red cooking." This simply means the meat is first deep-fried and then placed in a sweet-sour sauce.

Serves 4

1½ pound fresh whole fish
3 tablespoons cornstarch
  mixed with 2½ tablespoons
  water
4 cups vegetable oil
¾ cup pickled Chinese
  mixed vegetables (optional)

Clean the fish and make 3 or 4 diagonal slashes on each side from tail to head. Rub with the mixture of cornstarch and water. Heat the oil in a heavy pan to 350°. Slowly put the fish in the oil and fry 5 minutes on each side or until done. Remove the fish to platter and drain off any oil with absorbent paper. (If fish is too bulky for the pan, it may be cut diagonally into 2 sections for easy frying.)

Sauce:

1 tablespoon cornstarch
½ cup light brown sugar
⅓ cup cider vinegar, or red
  Chinese vinegar
⅓ cup water
1 teaspoon soy sauce

Combine the ingredients for the sauce and bring to a boil. Add the Chinese pickled vegetables and simmer for 30 seconds. Pour the sauce over the fish and serve at once.

Black Bean Butterfish

(Tao-see-yu)

豆豉魚

Westerners frequently pass by black beans because of their undistinguished appearance, but they are missing out if they do not try them. Lobster with black beans is one of the finest Cantonese dishes, and many who have tried it would attest to its tastiness.

Black beans when fermented become very soft. You may buy them in a Chinese grocery and they will keep unrefrigerated in a plastic box for up to three months.

Black beans are widely considered a food for the poor since they are very high in protein, inexpensive, and add much flavor to dishes that are mostly rice and little meat or vegetables. They are rarely served when entertaining except in such recipes as this one—with fish, shrimp, or lobster, with which they are ironically considered gourmet fare.
fare.

For the following recipe one may substitute any favorite type of fish. Just remember that black beans are quite salty and other salt, if needed, should be sparingly used.

Serves 2

2 tablespoons fermented black beans

Soak the beans in 2 cups hot tap water for 5 to 10 minutes. Transfer with the fingers to another 2 cups of hot tap water. This will wash any sand grains from them. Remove from the water and the beans are ready for use. (This process is used to make sure that all particles of sand are removed from beans before they are used.)

3 cloves garlic
¼ teaspoon sugar
¼ square inch fresh ginger root
¼ cup soy sauce
4 teaspoons oil

Finely chop and crush the garlic and ginger together, and fry them with the processed black beans and sugar in 2 teaspoons oil at medium heat for about 1 minute, stirring frequently. Mix with soy sauce and set aside.

1 pound fresh butterfish or other fish cut into segments
1 green onion, chopped

Put another 2 teaspoons oil in a clean frying pan and fry the fish for about 5 minutes per side or until the flesh flakes easily. Pour the sauce over the fish and cook for 30 seconds. Serve in a preheated platter with plain steamed rice and garnished with chopped green onion.

King Crab Curry

(Gar-lee-wong-hai)

咖喱王蟹

This is an excellent dish for busy people and for entertaining. It is amazingly quick to prepare, since little cooking is involved, yet is most colorful, has an excellent bouquet, and is on the spicy side, which breaks the monotony of the stir-fry dishes.

Serves 2

2 cloves garlic, peeled and crushed
4 inches green onion, white part only

Finely chop the garlic and green onion and place in a small bowl.

2 teaspoons peanut oil

Set a 14 to 16-inch wok or a large skillet over medium-high heat for about 30 seconds, then spread 2 teaspoons of oil over the surface with a spatula. Heat for another 30 seconds or until the oil begins to smoke. Add the garlic and onion mixture and stir about 10 seconds or until it produces a good aroma.

1 pound King Crab leg, with shell cut into 2-inch segments

Add the King Crab chunks and stir-fry for 2 minutes. Sprinkle the sherry or brandy around the edges of the wok or skillet and

2 teaspoons cooking sherry
  or brandy
½ cup chicken broth or fish
  broth

Seasoning:

1 teaspoon monosodium
  glutamate
1 teaspoon brown sugar
1 tablespoon curry powder or
  to taste
salt to taste
dash white pepper

½ cup milk or coconut milk
1½ teaspoons cornstarch
  mixed with 1½ teaspoons
  water
1 egg yolk, lightly beaten
  with a fork
2 tablespoons chopped green
  onions

add the broth and seasoning. Bring the sauce to a boil and add the milk. Bring the sauce to a boil again and stir in the cornstarch and water mixture, gradually, to form a gravy. Add the egg yolk and stir the sauce well. Transfer to a heated platter and sprinkle with the chopped green onion for decoration.

King Crab in Black Bean Sauce

(See-jop-wong-hai)

豉汁王蟹

Serves 2 to 4

4 teaspoons salted black
  beans
1 clove garlic, finely
  chopped
¼ square inch fresh ginger
  root, peeled and finely
  chopped

1 pound King Crab legs,
  cooked

1½ teaspoon cornstarch
  mixed with 1½ teaspoon
  water

Soak black beans in a small bowl with 1 cup warm water to cover for 15-20 minutes. Remove with fingers and place in another small bowl. Using the fingers, mix in the garlic and ginger to form a paste.

Cut up the crab legs, shell and all, into 2-inch pieces. Drain in a colander.

Prepare a thickening base from the cornstarch and water and set aside.

4 teaspoons vegetable oil

Heat the wok and using a spatula spread oil over a large area. When it begins to smoke, add the black beans and stir-fry until they emit a strong aroma — about 30 seconds. If overcooked, the black beans will taste bitter.

2 teaspoons cooking sherry
¾ cup chicken broth
¼ teaspoon monosodium glutamate
1 teaspoon sesame oil (optional)
dash of white pepper
½ teaspoon white sugar
½ egg yolk
1 tablespoon chopped green onions

Remove the black beans from the cooking area, add 2 teaspoons more oil if necessary, and sauté the crab. After 2-3 minutes, mix the black beans and crab. Mound in the center of the wok and add sherry. Add the chicken broth. Season to taste with monosodium glutamate, sesame oil, white pepper, and sugar. When the sauce comes to a rapid boil, add the thickening base, the egg yolk, and chopped green onions and mix well. Salt to taste.

Serve on a preheated platter.

Sizzling Rice

(Wor-bar)

The louder the noise, the better the cook. This favorite Northern Chinese dish may seem strange to the Occidental, but its creation reflects clever thinking. Because the Northern Chinese were unwilling to throw away the crusted rice left over in the wok, they devised a unique way to serve the crust. It is cut into pieces, deep-fried in a special sauce, and flavored with hot spices. The serving of this dish is something to behold, for hot sauce is integral to the presentation. When the sauce is poured over the rice, a sizzling sound is heard.

Serve this dish the next time you entertain, if you really want to catch everyone's attention.

Serves 4

4 cups long grain rice
6 cups water

Wash the long grain rice until the water is clear. Add to a wok with 6 cups of water. Stir the rice a bit so that the water will get to the bottom of the wok. Cover and bring to a boil. Simmer the rice for 45 minutes. The rice should be spread around the surface of the wok so that it can form a large crust on the bottom. When the rice is cooked, scoop the center of the cooked rice out of the wok, leaving the skin. Let stand in the wok for 15 minutes. Remove the crust from the wok with a spatula. Cut the rice crust into sections 1½ inches x 2 inches. Set aside.

Sauce:

2 cups chicken broth
1 tablespoon Worcestershire
** sauce**
½ teaspoon sugar
½ teaspoon sesame oil
½ teaspoon monosodium
** glutamate**
salt to taste
dash white pepper
1 teaspoon soy sauce
2 teaspoons oyster sauce
** (optional)**
1 cup catsup
tabasco to taste
2 teaspoons sherry
½ teaspoon salt

Thickening:

1 tablespoon cornstarch
** mixed with 1 tablespoon**
** water**

Prepare the sauce and thickening and set aside.

2 teaspoons vegetable oil
2 cloves garlic, chopped

Heat the wok. Add peanut oil (or other vegetable oil) and heat until the oil begins

2 tablespoons chopped green
  onion
½ pound pork, diced
½ pound shrimp, deveined
  and diced
½ cup sliced bamboo shoots
  (optional)

to smoke. Add the chopped garlic and green onion and sauté for 5-10 seconds until it produces a good aroma. Add the diced pork and fry for 2 minutes on each side. Add the shrimp. Fry for 1 minute on each side and add the sliced bamboo shoots, if desired. Pour in the prepared sauce and mix well. When it comes to a boil, stir in the thickening base of corn-starch and water. Transfer the sauce from the wok to a pot and keep it hot.

3 cups peanut oil

Heat 3 cups of oil to 350° in a wok or pot. Deep fry the rice crust pieces. The rice will sizzle in the hot oil until it expands to its maximum. Once the sizzling sound stops, remove the rice crust pieces and serve immediately.

Serve the rice crust pieces in small individual bowls. Pour hot sauce over the rice. If both the rice and the sauce are hot, the rice crust will sizzle with a singing sound and your dish is a success!

Poached Shrimp

(Jum-har)

浸蝦

Serves 4

1 pound large fresh shrimp
  (15-20 per pound)
2 square inches fresh ginger
  root, crushed
3 scallions, cut in half and
  crushed
red lettuce

Remove the legs from the shrimp, but do not peel. Fill a wok with enough boiling water to cover the shrimp by 2 inches. Add the crushed ginger and scallions. Boil rapidly for 10 minutes. Add the shrimp and stir to assure that the water is a uniform temperature. When the water is back to a boil, turn off the heat or remove the pan from the burner. Let stand for 5-7 minutes, then scoop out the shrimp and place them on a bed of red lettuce on a platter. If used as an appetizer, let the guests peel shrimp themselves and provide a small container for shells. Allow 4-5 shrimp per person.

The shrimp may be accompanied by one or more of the following as a dip:
1. 4-5 tablespoons soy sauce (yellow or thin soy sauce preferred) mixed with 1 tablespoon peanut oil and a dash of pepper and sesame oil
2. Oyster sauce
3. Catsup
4. 1 cup *hoi sin* sauce mixed with the juice of ½ fresh lemon

1 teaspoon *Mui Kwe Lu* **or brandy**

For aroma and an added touch to this famed dish from Hong Kong floating restaurants, add 1 teaspoon of *Mui Kwe Lu* (Chinese rose petal rice wine) to the shrimp on the serving platter. You may serve small hot towels in lieu of a finger bowl.

Deep Fried Oysters

(Jar-hsiang-ho)

炸生蠔

Serves 1 to 2

1 dozen chilled oysters, not frozen

Place the oysters in a colander and run water over them to wash away the fishy smell, guiding the flow by hand to prevent pressure from breaking up the oysters. Soak them in ½ cup milk for 2-4 hours in the refrigerator. Remove and drain, but keep wet.

---

2 egg yolks
1 cup milk
1 to 1½ cups cornstarch
1 to 1½ cups cracker crumbs

Beat the egg yolks in a small bowl with a fork and add the other ½ cup of milk. Dip the oysters in cornstarch, coating them well. Shake lightly and immerse them completely in the egg-milk mixture. Brush the oysters against the edge of a bowl so the mixture will not be too heavy. Roll them in cracker crumbs and put on a platter, separating the layers with wax paper. This may be done the night before cooking. Refrigerate for 2-4 hours to give a better taste and frying effect.

---

4 cups oil, preferably
 vegetable oil
1 cup shredded lettuce

Heat the oil to 350°. Test it with bread. Immerse the oysters one at a time, for 1½ to 2 minutes, or until golden. Salt oysters on removal and drain off oil with absorbent paper. Shred lettuce on a preheated platter, arrange the oysters on the lettuce, and serve. Catsup may be served as a dip.

Vegetables

There is no equivalent in the Chinese language for the word *salad*. In China, raw vegetables are not presented on the dining table. However, there are a number of dishes that may best be compared to the American salad, and these may be served as a main dish or as a salad in the familiar sense of uncooked greens mixed with some kind of dressing.

Chicken Salad

(Sau-see-gai)

手撕雞

This chicken dish is one that is readily accepted by both Chinese and Americans, and it is so versatile that it can be served as a salad or entree.

The secret of this recipe is the Chinese red vinegar that is used in the dressing. Sometimes it is available in large grocery stores or specialty shops. If you cannot find it nearby, it can be easily packed and shipped by most suppliers. In the last 16 years I have cooked in nearly every state including Alaska and have had little difficulty in securing the ingredients necessary for any of the dishes I prepare.

One interesting variation on this recipe is to use turkey, abalone, and cooked ham instead of the chicken for the meat. The dish would then be called "Sam See Salad." *Sam see* means three different kinds of cooked meats cut into strips.

Serves 2

2 cups cooked chicken meat

Marinade:

½ **teaspoon monosodium glutamate**
½ **teaspoon sugar**
½ **teaspoon sesame oil**
½ **teaspoon salt**
dash white pepper
2 teaspoons oyster sauce
2 teaspoons soy sauce
1 teaspoon peanut or vege-table oil
3 teaspoons dry sherry
2 tablespoons Chinese red vinegar
tabasco to taste

Use chicken that has been deep-fried, roasted, or boiled, but not barbecued. Cut the meat into 2-inch strips about ¼-inch thick. Combine the chicken with marinade ingredients and mix well, then let it sit for at least ½ hour.

Vegetables:

2 cups head lettuce
½ cup green onion
1 cup celery

2 cups Chinese *won bok* **cabbage or Romaine lettuce**
1 bunch Chinese parsley (optional)

Dressing:

½ teaspoon monosodium glutamate
½ teaspoon sugar
½ teaspoon salt
1 teaspoon sesame oil
1 teaspoon soy sauce
¼ teaspoon tabasco
¼ teaspoon pepper
1 tablespoon oyster sauce
⅓ cup Chinese red vinegar
¼ cup salted peanuts, crushed finely
Roasted sesame seeds

Slice the lettuce and *won bok* into thin strips about ¼-inch wide and 2-inches long. Cut the green onion into thin strips, about 1½ inches in length and also cut the celery into thin pieces, julienne style. Cut Chinese parsley in 2-inch sprigs.

Gently mix the vegetables and dressing in a large salad bowl. Add the chicken and half of the peanuts and again gently mix well. Transfer onto a platter and garnish with the remainder of the peanuts and roasted sesame seeds. Do not mix the salad with the seasonings until just before serving since the vegetables will then wilt rather rapidly and the salad will lose its texture.

Poached Watercress

(Jum-sai-yong-choy)

浸西洋菜

Serves 2 as a side dish

2 bunches watercress, washed
2 teaspoons vegetable oil
dash white pepper
salt to taste
8-10 cups hot water

Fill a pot with water and bring to a rapid boil. Grasp a bunch of watercress by the stem part and dip the leaf portion completely into boiling water for 3 seconds. Remove and cool for 5 seconds. Repeat the process five times or until done to taste. Repeat with the second bunch.

Drain and brush the watercress with oil for a shiny effect. Cut the cooked leafy portion into 2-inch segments. Serve warm or cold.

Cucumber Salad

(Wong-gua)

黄瓜沙律

Actually the Chinese do not consider this a "salad" but a simple vegetable dish that is easily made and refreshing on a hot day. Cucumber is one of the few vegetables eaten fresh without cooking in China—largely because of the way most vegetables are fertilized. As in this recipe the seeds are usually scooped out first.

Serves 4 to 6 as a side dish

3 medium cucumbers

Peel cucumbers lengthwise in alternate strips to create a striped green-white effect. Cut off the ends of the cucumbers then slice in half, length-wise. Scoop out seeds from each half and slice into half-moons ¼-inch thick.

¼ cup soy sauce
1 teaspoon sesame oil
3 tablespoons light brown sugar
3 tablespoons cider vinegar
salt and pepper to taste
parsley

Mix the remaining ingredients and toss the cucumbers 3-5 minutes before serving. Garnish with parsley.

Desserts

The Chinese have never had the Western-style gelatin but have made use of a similar substance derived from vegetation called *"leung fun cho,"* or from aga aga. Dessert in the Western sense is not found in the dictionary of real cuisine of old Cathay. Frequently, orange wedges, or other fresh fruits are served at the conclusion of a meal at formal dinners, but if not served, dessert is not missed. Perhaps if there are fewer overweight Chinese than Westerners, it is because of the absence of these extra calories.

Almond Float

(Hung-yun-je-lei)

杏仁啫喱

Once you try this dish, however, you will wonder that desserts are not a specialty of the Chinese. It is simple, light, and indescribably delicious. What more could one ask of a dessert?

Serves 6 to 8

2 packages unflavored gelatin
1 cup and 3 tablespoons cold water
1 tablespoon almond extract
1 cup milk
¾ cup sugar

Sprinkle gelatin in 3 tablespoons cold water to soften. Bring 1 cup of water to a boil, add the gelatin, and stir well until dissolved. Add milk, sugar, and almond extract. Pour the mixture into a wet, flat 5 x 11-inch pan and refrigerate.

12 laichi, canned or fresh
5 cherries, halved, or ½ cup diced peaches, canned or fresh

If fresh fruits are used, make a simple syrup by boiling ½ cup sugar and 2 cups water together. If canned fruits are used, use the fruit's syrup.

Dice the almond gelatin into diamond shapes and add the syrup and fruits.

Where to Buy It

Chong Kee Jan Company
838 Grant Avenue
San Francisco, California 94108

Dupont Market
1100 Grant Avenue
San Francisco, California 94133

Ginn Wall Company
1016 Grant Avenue
San Francisco, California 94133

Hong Kong Town
2228 South Wentworth
Chicago, Illinois 60616

House of Rice
4112 University Way, N.E.
Seattle, Washington 98105
(No catalogue available)

Kam Shing Company
2246 Wentworth Avenue
Chicago, Illinois 60616
(C.O.D. orders must be $20.00 or more)

Mon Fong Wo Company
36 Pell Street
New York, New York 10013

Tai Yen Company
1023 Maunakea Street
Honolulu, Hawaii 96817

Tuck Cheong Company
617 H Street, N.W.
Washington, D.C. 20001

Wang's Company
800 7th Street, N.W.
Washington, D.C. 20001

Wing Sing Chong Company, Inc.
921-931 Clay Street
San Francisco, California 94108

Glossary

Bamboo shoots. Cone-shaped shoots of the bamboo plant; they can be purchased in cans and are normally about 3x4 inches in size and ivory-colored. Those packed in water are best and should be refrigerated in water after opening.

Bar gok. A Chinese herb called *star anise* in English. In its natural state, it is an 8-pointed star, 1 inch across.

Bean sauce. A thick sauce made from fermented yellow beans, flour, and salt. Bottled or canned, it will last a few months under refrigeration and adds a salty taste to gravies and sauces.

Black beans. Salty fermented black soybeans; they are sold in plastic bags. They add both flavor and aroma and are frequently used in combination with ginger and garlic.

Buck kay. Chinese medicinal herb. It is a white root usually about three inches in length and about ½ inch wide.

Char siu. Marinated roast pork, which, due to the marinade, is bright red in color. It can usually be found in any Chinese meat market.

Chinese parsley. Fresh coriander or cilantro, to Occidentals, a strong-flavored vegetable somewhat flatter than Western parsley. Sold fresh in bunches in grocery stores.

Cho quor. Also known as *grass fruit.* A small dried fruit that looks like a pecan and is used as an herb to add aroma to dishes. It has a mild flavor, but strong aroma, somewhat similar to the seed of a citrus fruit.

Chung choy. Salted preserved sliced turnips, which are used to add a salty, pungent taste to various dishes and soups.

Dong sum. Medicinal herb in root form, similar to *ginseng,* which is frequently used with *buck kay.* Believed to aid circulation. Purchased in herb stores.

Gai choy. Chinese mustard cabbage; leafy portion has slightly bitter taste. Deep green in color, also called *mustard green.*

Gay gee. Red dried seed about the size of a wheat grain, used to add sweetness to dishes. A popular herb with Chinese women.

Heong liu fun (Chinese Five Spice Powder). A combination of five powdered spices, light yellow in color. Used to add aroma or marinate roast meat such as *char siu.* Consists of fennel, clove, cinnamon, anise, and Szechuan pepper.

Hoi sin sauce. Sweet, pungent, thick brown sauce made from fermented yellow beans, sugar, garlic, red rice, salt, flour, and water. Used in cooking or as a dip for roast duck and other meats.

Hok. Long-handled ladle used in cooking. Bowl of ladle is usually about 5 inches in diameter (but varies) and the handle may be about one foot or more in length.

Laichi. Small fruit borne on trees, which resembles a strawberry at first glance but has a rough red skin covering white meat and a large brown pit. May be purchased fresh or dried, or in cans. The flesh of the fruit is similar to a grape in texture and flavor.

Lily flower. Dried lily buds 2-3 inches in length and pale gold in color. When cooked with meats and other vegetables, it functions as a "borrower," soaking up other flavors.

Long rice. Actually made from ground mung beans rather than rice, these are long translucent noodles that are purchased dried in packages. Sometimes called *cellophane noodles.*

Lotus root. Long root 2-3 inches in diameter with sausage-like segments about 6 inches in length. When sliced, each piece has holes like Swiss cheese. It may be purchased fresh, canned, or dried.

Mui kwe lu. 96 proof distilled white rice wine prized for its aroma and flavor when used in cooking. Sometimes called *rose wine,* since it is flavored with rose petals.

Ng ka py. 96 proof distilled red spirits used chiefly for drinking.

Oyster sauce. Made from oysters, soy sauce, and brine, this thick brown sauce is used very widely to enhance the taste of all types of dishes—meats and vegetables.

Plum sauce. Sweet brown sauce made from plums, apricots, vinegar, sugar, and chili. It is very tasty and used as a dip for duck and other meats.

Rice sticks. Brittle white noodles similar to long rice but especially good for deep frying, whereas long rice is usually soaked in water.

Sam ching. 73.8 proof clear distilled spirits used both for drinking and for medicinal purposes.

Sar gen (sand ginger). Form of ginger used as an herb, dried and thinly sliced.

Soy sauce. Made from fermented soy beans, yeast, salt, and wheat, this pungent brown sauce is usually quite thin and is used in cooking and flavoring all types of dishes.

Taro. Large potato-like tuber that is used in cooking much like potatoes or sweet potatoes. May be purchased fresh in grocery stores.

Tofu. Pureed soybeans are pressed into square cakes with an appearance similar to custard. Very high in protein, they add body and flavor to many meat and vetetable dishes.

Wai son. Medicinal herb used frequently with *gay gee*.

Water chestnut. Round bulb that grows in water. The skin is tough and dark brown or purplish, while the flesh is crisp and white. It is used to add flavor and texture to meat and vegetable dishes and may be bought fresh or in cans, in which case it may be whole, diced, or sliced. It may be eaten raw.

Wok. The primary instrument of Chinese cooking, the wok takes the place of frying pan, pot, or double-boiler. It is round, usually 14-18 inches in diameter (for home use), with a rounded bottom, as if it were a section sliced from a sphere.

Wok cheun. Chinese long-handled spatula used in cooking along with a hok and wok. The spatula is usually about 4-5 inches wide, with a handle 1 inch or more in length.

Won bok. Chinese cabbage, which is similar to celery in appearance but its stalks are white and smooth, lacking the fibers of celery. Won bok may be used in meat and vegetable dishes or in salads.

Yuen yok. Dried flesh of a fruit similar to laichi. Purchased in herb stores, it enhances the sweetness of a dish. Also called *dragon eye*.

Index

R

S